The Teaching Librarian

CHANDOS
INFORMATION PROFESSIONAL SERIES

Series Editor: Ruth Rikowski
(email: Rikowskigr@aol.com)

Chandos' new series of books is aimed at the busy information professional. They have been specially commissioned to provide the reader with an authoritative view of current thinking. They are designed to provide easy-to-read and (most importantly) practical coverage of topics that are of interest to librarians and other information professionals. If you would like a full listing of current and forthcoming titles, please visit our website, www.chandospublishing.com, email wp@woodheadpublishing.com or telephone +44 (0) 1223 499140.

New authors: we are always pleased to receive ideas for new titles; if you would like to write a book for Chandos, please contact Dr Glyn Jones on gjones@chandospublishing.com or telephone +44 (0) 1993 848726.

Bulk orders: some organisations buy a number of copies of our books. If you are interested in doing this, we would be pleased to discuss a discount. Please email wp@woodheadpublishing.com or telephone +44 (0) 1223 499140.

The Teaching Librarian

Web 2.0, technology, and legal aspects

KRIS HELGE AND LAURA F. MCKINNON

CP

CHANDOS
PUBLISHING

Oxford Cambridge New Delhi

Chandos Publishing
Hexagon House
Avenue 4
Station Lane
Witney
Oxford OX28 4BN
UK
Tel: +44 (0) 1993 848726
Email: info@chandospublishing.com
www.chandospublishing.com
www.chandospublishingonline.com

Chandos Publishing is an imprint of Woodhead Publishing Limited

Woodhead Publishing Limited
80 High Street
Sawston
Cambridge CB22 3HJ
UK
Tel: +44 (0) 1223 499140
Fax: +44 (0) 1223 832819
www.woodheadpublishing.com

First published in 2013

ISBN: 978-1-84334-733-0 (print)
ISBN: 978-1-78063-399-2 (online)

Chandos Information Professional Series ISSN: 2052-210X (print) and ISSN: 2052-2118 (online)

Library of Congress Control Number: 2013948662

British Library Cataloguing-in-Publication Data.
A catalogue record for this book is available from the British Library.

Typeset by Domex e-Data Pvt. Ltd., India
Printed in the UK and USA.

Laura – To Kevin, with all my love.
Kris – To Terri, Andrew, Jason, Jacob, Emelie, and Mom
with love for the most important things in life.

Contents

List of abbreviations

ACS	affective computing software
APA	American Psychological Association
ATN	augmented transition network
CC	Creative Commons
CSS	content scrambling system
IaaS	infrastructure as a service
MIT	Massachusetts Institute of Technology
MLA	Modern Language Association
OCW	Open Course Ware program
PaaS	platform as a service
PDF	portable document format
QR	quick response
RSS	Rich Site Summary
S3	Simple Storage Service
SaaS	software as a service
SCORM	sharable content object reference model
SL	Second Life

SPARC	Scholarly Publishing and Academic Resources Coalition
SSL	Secure Sockets Layer
TEACH	Technology, Education, and Copyright Harmonization Act
VoIP	voice over internet protocol

About the authors

Kris Helge is the scholarly communications librarian at the University of North Texas, where he advises and teaches people about copyright, open access, and the use of Web 2.0 tools in their pedagogy. He earned a BA from Baylor University, a JD from South Texas College of Law, and an MLS from the University of North Texas, and is a PhD student at the University of North Texas. Prior to working at the University of North Texas, he served as a law librarian at the Baylor Law School and the University of Texas Wesleyan School of Law, where he taught multiple advanced legal research classes and implemented Web 2.0 technology in his pedagogy. He is the author of numerous articles pertaining to the law.

Laura F. McKinnon is head of the research and instructional services department at the University of North Texas Willis Library. Prior to this, she served as a public services librarian at the Dee J. Kelly Law Library at Texas Wesleyan School of Law, where she taught advanced legal research classes and implemented Web 2.0 technology in her pedagogy. She earned a BS from the University of Florida, a JD from Florida State University College of Law, and an MLIS from Florida State University College of Information.

Web 2.0 tools: benefits, detriments, and usage for effective pedagogy

Abstract: This chapter defines and identifies the differences between Web 1.0 and Web 2.0 tools. It describes how various Web 2.0 tools may be used in pedagogical guises: examples are given for wikis, Moodles, Camtasia, Facebook, Second Life, Adobe Connect, YouTube, and Mindomo. Additionally, some empirical studies are briefly mentioned that have exemplified the pedagogical benefits of these tools. The chapter conveys the importance of choosing a Web 2.0 tool that logically fits with the substantive topical goals of teaching librarians and students. The tool selected should also offer equal access, improve communication, provide an adequate level of class organization, and meet the needs of traditional and non-traditional students.

Key words: Web 1.0, Web 2.0, pedagogy, Second Life, wiki, Mindomo, Moodle, Camtasia, Facebook, Google+, YouTube, cost effective, equal access, non-traditional students, organization.

Introduction

Today, more and more people communicate via social media such as Facebook, Twitter, Google+ and other electronic forums. And many prefer to obtain their music from

YouTube, iTunes, or some other intangible medium rather than listening to CDs or the radio. As technologies that transmit music or foster efficient communication between people continue to evolve rapidly, it is important that teaching librarians keep pace with these changes and utilize current preferred technologies in their pedagogical endeavors. By using emerging and contemporary technologies, teaching librarians are likely to catch students' interests and subsequently spark creative abilities in these students; whereas teaching librarians who continue to embrace the traditional passive lecture/note-taking model will not foster creative thinking and deep-level learning in today's classes. Thus it is important that teaching librarians become familiar with and embrace Web 2.0 and eventually Web 3.0 tools in their pedagogy. This book discusses various Web 2.0 tools such as wikis, Facebook, LibGuides, apps, and others. Additionally, some emerging Web 3.0 tools are discussed that teaching librarians should be on the lookout for to implement in their pedagogical endeavors in the near future.

Difference between Web 1.0 and Web 2.0

In the early part of this millennium, the web witnessed an evolution from Web 1.0 to Web 2.0 tools. Web 1.0 is defined as a one-way communication presented on websites, and is primarily used for proprietary interests; Web 2.0 is defined as websites or web tools that offer two-way communications between information presented on the website and the user.[1] In other words, Web 2.0 tools and sites are dynamic and allow users to interact with and modify the content on that tool or site. An example of a Web 1.0 site is Pete's Garage website, which is static; it simply communicates prices and hours of operation of its business, and does not offer any means by which users of the site may interact with or alter the site in any guise. An example of a Web 2.0 site is a wiki such as Wikipedia. A wiki is dynamic: viewers may interact with, communicate, and alter the content placed on a wiki. Thus Web 2.0 tools offer an environment with rich tools that create potential learning opportunities and encourage active rather than passive student interaction with the website. Web 2.0 sites foster learning and active interaction by forcing students to look critically at the content located on the site, attempt to interact with the content, and then synthesize the information and make appropriate additions or modifications. Thus ultimately Web 2.0 sites catalyze deeper-level learning in students than do Web 1.0 sites.

Importance of using Web 2.0 tools

Utilizing and offering Web 2.0 technologies in pedagogy provide a panoply of benefits to students and teaching librarians. For example, empirical research has demonstrated that using Web 2.0 tools such as Facebook, Mindomo, Camtasia, Second Life, wikis, YouTube, and other rich-text formats augments pedagogy by producing deep-level learning in students.[2] Web 2.0 technologies encourage deeper-level learning because they offer rich-text learning venues in which collaboration, independent thought and creation, and asynchronous work sharing flourish.[3] Such actions foster student metacognition (thinking about and questioning what one is learning), constructive peer review, and critical thinking, all of which in turn foster synthesis of new knowledge.[4] Promoting these cognitive activities also encourages the highest levels of student learning, such as synthesis of various types of information.[5] Synthesizing new knowledge is what creates long-term memory of information. Thus the more teaching librarians can utilize Web 2.0 tools, the better they can equip students with information, knowledge, and wisdom they will perpetually retain. Students retain this learned knowledge due to the Web 2.0 tools fostering of critical thinking, synthesis of information to create long-term knowledge, and creativity.

Unfortunately, many academies in the United Kingdom and the United States do not utilize Web 2.0 tools and instead partake in educational endeavors detrimental to student development that only contribute to surface-level learning. Surface-level learning consists of offering new concepts to students only long enough for them to regurgitate these concepts in a test a few days later. Surface-level pedagogy creates a lack of integrating new concepts with stored knowledge, and thus results in a complete absence of synthesizing the new information with stored knowledge to create new knowledge.[6] Yet if educators embrace tools such as Second Life, Facebook, wikis, and YouTube, student collaboration occurs, which promotes a self- and team teaching effect[7] and cooperation, benefits all the learning styles, and leads to a deeper level of learning.[8] Deep-level learning stimulates active memorization that fosters critical thought about the new content, and an ability to connect this new information to already-stored cognitive knowledge which leads to the synthesis of new information or knowledge.

Teaching librarians' roles in using Web 2.0 technologies

The older pedagogical model of librarian instructors serving as lecturers is changing with the pervasion of Web 2.0 tools. As this model evolves, the librarian instructor now serves as a guide or facilitator rather than as a lecturer. This new model allows librarians to pre-record lectures, PowerPoints, and other course notes; and post these to a class blog, wiki, distance-learning module, Facebook, or some other Web 2.0 tool. Students view or listen to these pre-recorded renditions prior to class, and then are allowed to experiment with and implement their newly gained knowledge in a face-to-face class or a virtual class setting. While students are testing this new knowledge, the teaching librarian offers a sterile venue in which students may experiment without fear of failure because they will not face a deleterious ramification, and ultimately encourages students to synthesize pre-learned information with newly learned information so they may retain, evaluate, synthesize, and apply the new information.[9]

Students' roles with Web 2.0 tools

By being given this sterile educational environment, students have an opportunity to learn how to use Web 2.0 tools efficiently and manage technological glitches; take advantage of their rich-text learning environment; and implement them to co-create with other students, share rich information (such as audio files, audio-visual information, links to information...), effectively communicate with peers and the instructor, and learn to decipher what is proper and not proper to post in various types of digital environments. Thus a student's primary tasks when interacting with Web 2.0 tools consist of using these tools enough to become comfortable with them, modifying the tools or the content they convey, critiquing the content presented, and synthesizing the information presented with the student's stored knowledge to create original thought or new information.

Empirical research showing benefits of Web 2.0 learning

Empirical studies exemplify the above-mentioned pedagogical benefits for students and teaching librarians when utilizing Web 2.0 tools in the classroom. Davis and Loasby empirically demonstrated how using such tools in pedagogy increased student engagement and learning.[10] These instructors assigned their students to groups to use Web 2.0 technology while writing a study guide for a chapter, which promoted deeper levels of perception and learning. Such an assignment encourages students to create drafts of a work product, participate in peer review of other students' work, and think critically about their own work product, the work product of their peers, and their body of work as a whole. In other words, offering such an assignment in concert with a Web 2.0 technology fosters crucial metacognition that ultimately leads to higher levels of learning. These levels of learning foster synthesis of new knowledge. It is difficult to replicate such metacognition and the synthesis of new knowledge in a pedagogical environment that only offers the traditional lecture note-taking format.

This type of pedagogical format utilizing Web 2.0 tools could be replicated by librarians teaching any substantive topic. For example, law librarians could assign groups of law students to use a wiki to create a model statute regarding theft and a hypothetical example where it may apply, and draft a brief transcript of a trial where one could be prosecuted with the model statute. Subsequently, the students could film a mock trial using the transcript they created, and post the trial to YouTube. Such an educational endeavor provides a rich context for all learner styles to apply new knowledge.

Alternatively, a teaching librarian can use a wiki and embed videos that catch students' attention. While garnering attention, these videos can convey pedagogical substantive content such as how to utilize an electronic database, how to cite electronic or print materials, and how to upload educational content on to a site such as YouTube. By catching students' attention with these Web 2.0 tools, teaching librarians may then encourage them to think critically about the substantive content being offered, which in turn fosters metacognitive processes.

Using specific Web 2.0 tools in pedagogy

Using a wiki in pedagogy

The use of wikis in academic instruction produces many of the above-mentioned pedagogical benefits, but also some detriments. Varga-Atkins et al. empirically studied medical students at the University of Liverpool who implemented wikis in pedagogy.[11] These researchers discovered that students were more likely to discuss work-related issues and share professional resources on a wiki than on Facebook because they perceived Facebook as a social tool and a wiki as being designated for work. Additionally, most students posted web links on the wiki rather than a narrative. Thus it may behoove teaching librarians to advise students to utilize the wiki as a formal class discussion tool to convey related substantive content, share class-related links and resources, post class-content-related videos and images, and have any other class-related material exchanges. Further, the teaching librarian may want to provide a class Facebook page for students so they have access to an informal site as well.

Thus teaching librarians may want to offer a wiki to students for multiple uses.

- As an information repository where students feel comfortable sharing class-content-related knowledge.
- As an information repository to share class-related videos and images.
- As information repositories that can save students time as they review information already posted by another student.
- To save students time by reviewing all the posted information prior to going to class.
- As a repository to post lectures, narratives, or other information so that students can view or listen to this material prior to class. Such pre-viewing or listening can allow students to commence hands-on activities immediately when arriving at class, thus saving students and instructors time. Further, in this guise instructors are able to serve more as a guide than as a lecturer.

Because students may still prefer to have access to a class-related site where they can opine informal information, it may behoove a teaching librarian to offer an additional Web 2.0 tool on which such informal discussions may occur. Thus an instructor may want to implement a wiki and a Web 2.0 tool such as Facebook or Google+. If these two separate tools are utilized, the wiki is viewed as a professional tool and Facebook or Google+ is perceived as more of a social tool. By giving students these opposite digital venues, they will learn how to remain cognizant of the importance of remaining professional when posting to an information repository, and also have access to a digital environment in which they can informally discuss study meeting times, ask questions about class they do not want the professor seeing, or even discuss unrelated class material such as with whom they just broke up. Some tips regarding how to set up and implement congruently used wikis and Facebook or Google+ are as follows.

- Set up a class Facebook or Google+ page that a professor is able to view and edit if necessary, but that he or she assures students is a safe space where all student postings will not adversely affect their grade regardless of grammar, syntax, or content.

- However, warn students that any offensive postings, postings that violate copyright, plagiarism, etc. will be removed; repetitive postings after being warned to stop inappropriate posts may negatively affect their grade.

- On the class Facebook site give students freedom to discuss issues not pertinent to the content of the class, such as what they did last weekend, who they are dating, and materials from other classes.

- Giving students this autonomy helps them learn in which venues it is appropriate to post formal professional material, and in which digital environments it is acceptable to post informal non-pertinent palaver.

- Set up a wiki in which students are directed only to post professional links, professional narratives, videos, audio material, etc.

- Provide students with clear and concise instructions as to the expected use for each forum (e.g. Facebook = acceptable informal discussions; wiki = only substantive class palaver).

- Educate students about plagiarism and copyright infringement, and warn them not to commit either lest they face grade deductions if they repeatedly commit these offenses.

- Allocate point deductions in the syllabus for posting informal content in the wiki after a predetermined number of specific warnings.

Organization is key – instructors' use of wikis

Proper organization of a wiki interface is vital. An empirical study found wikis provide excellent platforms on which to place course tools when they are properly organized.[12] However, if instructors place information on a wiki in a disjointed fashion, student learning will suffer. Students will begin querying 'where do I look for my assignment, grades...' and become frustrated, and such frustrations can lead to reticence and antagonism to learning.[13] Yet if an electronic syllabus links to content correlated to the course subject, such as MP3 files, web narratives, and videos, and teaching evaluations, course assignments, and communication venues are appropriately organized, then wikis are well liked and used by students, and are more likely to enhance student learning.

Here are some tips on how to organize a wiki.

- Place links to all pedagogical content on the homepage, e.g. place links to the syllabus, student grades, course assignments, discussion areas, etc. all via the homepage.

- Do not place two tools on the same page, as this will cause confusion, e.g. placing the discussion board on the same page as an archive link to videos. Place multiple links to items on the homepage, but not multiple items on the homepage.

- Do not place unnecessary information on a wiki just to fill space, e.g. do not place links to articles on an already crowded discussion board. Instead, if the articles are pertinent, email links or titles to students and have them retrieve the articles.

- Do not add random content to a wiki, or new wiki pages as the academic term progresses, without providing detailed explanation to students as to the purpose of this new content and how to access it quickly; and give clear and obvious links to the new material.

- If you are going to use a wiki as the main venue for class activities, try to stick to just this wiki, or limit your pedagogy to two Web 2.0 tools. Try not to set up a blog for class discussion as well, or another course forum such as Blackboard on which discussion will be held or documents viewed, or a Google Docs page on which other course content will be viewed. Having one site for all content relates back to good organization and student frustration. The more sites a student has to search to locate needed information, the more frustrated he/she is likely to become. Try to pick just one or two Web 2.0 tools (e.g. a wiki and Facebook), and offer all course content on those venues. In other words, do not use technology for technology's sake, use it for the benefit of students.

How a face-to-face class can augment the use of a wiki

Many academies offer classes that meet 100 percent online. Providing a venue for online instruction and collaboration is useful to students and teaching librarians. For example, online classes provide asynchronous learning, the elimination of geographical boundaries to education, removal of time barriers for students who work full- or part-time, and the general convenience to students of learning in their time and not when an academy mandates they should access pedagogical content.

Adding some face-to-face interaction also benefits learning by offering students a venue in which they may present projects, share theses and ideas, and practice skills they have synthesized or developed during the academic term. In other words, students are given the opportunity to implement in person what they have learned online. Within this face-to-face venue, students' peers and an instructor may provide in-person suggestions and constructive feedback, and students may more readily receive feedback than they would online. For example, a student who is learning how to create a LibGuide to offer access to medical sources could post such a guide to a wiki or a course module and allow his or her peers to view it and offer asynchronous comments, criticisms, and suggestions. However, by also presenting this guide in person to a live, synchronized audience, the student can show more features, synchronously react to the audience's responses, immediately change course or pace based on the audience reaction, and may also perceive audience feedback better, as 65 percent of all communication has been found to be non-verbal.[14] Thus by seeing the face of a peer or the librarian while obtaining a suggestion, the presenter is better able to decipher whether this suggestion is being offered out of genuine criticism, mere puffing, vehement dislike, or boredom. Being able to perceive such non-verbal cues can enable a presenter to know whether to tweak his or her idea or thesis, ignore the comment, or make additions or subtractions. Zhang and Olfman[15] found that students greatly valued the chance to interact in this way with their peers and instructor because the hands-on opportunities kept up their motivation to persist with outside lectures, they enjoyed the face-to-face collaborations and exchange of ideas, and it gave them plenty of time to consult with the instructor and their peers if they faced a problem they could not solve outside of class. Thus depending on the geographic location of students taking a course using online modules and Web 2.0 technology, a teaching librarian may use any of the following to serve as a guide to implementing face-to-face pedagogy.

- Offer half the pedagogical instruction face to face (e.g. meet online every other week).
- Meet face to face three weekends during the course term (three separate Saturdays and Sundays).
- Meet at least two weekends of the course term face to face (e.g. a Saturday and Sunday about halfway through the course, and a Saturday and Sunday toward the completion of term).
- Meet face to face for one weekend during the course term.
- Meet face to face for one week during the academic term (Monday through Friday).
- If geography is an insoluble barrier (e.g. face-to-face meeting is in London and a student resides in Los Angeles, another student's domicile is in Japan...), have one face-to-face meeting on a consecutive Saturday-Sunday format for those students who can meet in London, and implement Skype or videoconferencing for those who cannot surpass geographical barriers. A student Skyping in or videoconferencing can at least perceive some of the non-verbal cues he or she would surely miss in an online format.

Learning and cost effectiveness of a wiki

Rick et al. empirically examined whether using a wiki was both learning and cost effective by examining two separate English composition classes, and defined learning effectiveness as "the amount of information learned in relation to the cost for achieving it".[16] Their results suggested a group of students with access to a wiki moderately outperformed a group of students that did not have such access. Research conducted by Noveck corroborated these findings, suggesting wikis were designed to foster collective work and used based on the assumption that in certain circumstances the judgment of many was better than the judgment of a few.[17] Research completed by Achterman further supported this collectivist theory, and suggested that using wikis in academic settings allowed students to share easily and learn how to create products, edit them, and offer and reflect upon constructive criticism.[18] Such collaboration catalyzed by wikis provided deep levels of learning.[19] From these studies, one may reason that using a wiki justifies the cost considering the academic benefit to students. The cost and various features of some wikis that augment pedagogy are discussed below.

- *PB Works* (*http://pbworks.com/*). This wiki allows users to embed videos and links, and post messages, PowerPoints, documents, and links to outside sources; assists with distance learning; and encourages collaboration. Using the wiki, students can easily share created information with specific peers, the instructor, or the entire class in just seconds. The interface offers instructors three usage options: a Basic edition which is free; a Classroom edition which costs US$99 (£63) annually, gives the instructor more control over who may see and edit the content on the wiki, and allows a school branding on the course wiki; and the Campus edition, generally used by instructors teaching multiple classes with a wiki, which offers workspaces for numerous users and costs $799 (£510). PB Works also offers various business-specific hubs with which professionals may network. For example, Legal

Hub allows users to manage cases, perform necessary communications, and share relevant information. This feature could be beneficial to law students in their future information management and sharing endeavors. PB Works is portable between PCs and Macs.

- *Wetpaint Wikis in Education (http://wikisineducation. wetpaint.com/).* This site offers a nuts-and-bolts package in which instructors may create a class wiki or allow students to create their own. Wetpaint allows students to share created wiki pages, links, audio files, and audio-visual materials. It offers ad-free wikis on payment of an upgrade fee: an instructor can use Wetpaint free for pedagogical purposes, or choose an ad-free wiki for US$19.95 (£12.75) per month.

- *Wikispaces (www.wikispaces.com/).* Wikispaces is a free open source wiki with which instructors may enhance their pedagogical endeavors. Wikispaces is portable to personal computers, tablets, and smartphones. It allows instructors and students to create or add content such as calendars, videos, links to webpages, and audio files. Wikispaces provides a page history for the instructor so he or she may track what and when changes were made, and who completed them. This wiki offers free unlimited page usage, email notification, page templates, and full-text searching.

Moodle

Moodle (*https://moodle.org/*) is an acronym for Modular Object-Oriented Dynamic Learning Environment. It also is a verb meaning to meander lazily through a task.[20] Moodles are open source course management systems and similar to wikis, yet they offer different tools. They can support classes designed for ten to 30 students, like wikis, or many more students. Thus a university could theoretically utilize a Moodle for its entire online class platform, or it could be used to supplement a face-to-face-style class with only ten students or fewer.

Using a Moodle, teaching librarians and students can organize different pages for different content. Similar to using a wiki, instructors may place class calendars, discussion pages, links to MP3 lectures and videos, and assignment and course descriptions on separate pages within a class Moodle. Links to each of these topical pages can also be placed on the Moodle homepage. Having this accessibility and organization is helpful, and being open source the Moodle is free, unlike the commercial online educational venue providers.

Empirical research on Moodle

Moodles are relatively new Web 2.0 tools, thus there is not an abundance of empirical research regarding them. However, one empirical study illustrated the educational benefits of utilizing a Moodle in pedagogy: Henninger and Kutter at the University of Education Weingarten compared the use of a Moodle and a traditional online course management system called Distance Learning System 10.0.[21] Additionally, using a pre-test and post-test methodology, Md Ali and Jaafar attempted to discover whether using a Moodle to teach Malaysian undergraduates how to speak French would improve student learning compared to traditional lectures and hands-on interaction.[22] Both studies found that using a Moodle moderately increased student performance.

Benefits of using a Moodle

The usage of Moodles presents the potential of other pedagogical benefits as well. For example, Moodles can provide a range of content and many courses to one student or thousands of students. Moodles were developed to promote collaboration among students and an instructor, which in turn invites critical thought, peer review and other types of metacognition such as group presentation of ideas and discussion, reflection, and active learning. Such metacognition generally results in higher levels of learning and synthesis of new information. Moodles allow students and teaching librarians to post efficiently and have access to various forms of information – webpages, eBooks, forums, assignments, quizzes, databases, and glossaries.[23] Moodle formats are also available in over 100 different languages.[24]

Varied Moodle formats

Moodle offers a variety of attractive course formats, such as weekly, topics, social, and SCORM (sharable content object reference model) formats.[25] Each format allows teaching librarians to select a digital arrangement that best fits their pedagogical intent. For example, the topics format offers a template on which teaching librarians may offer topics that are stair stepped and build upon one another in a logical order. Thus a teaching librarian giving instruction about locating, retrieving, and citing an article from a database could logically organize and present topics such as using database search interfaces, locating PDFs, using internal database reference tools, and uploading proper citation. The topics format on the Moodle allows a teaching librarian to present these to students in a logical way.

Moodle training

Another advantage to Moodle is that users can download the software and immediately set up a course site and begin to add course content. For those needing assistance setting up a site in Moodle, or adding course content such as videos, links, or other information, Moodle offers a search site (*https://moodle.org/support/commercial/*) that will match users up with a valid and reliable technology partner to assist with the implementation and understanding of Moodle services. Such a partner may assist with developing the site, training individuals how to use the features, and answering any maintenance questions. Partners in the United States include Classroom Revolution, Moodlerooms, and Remote-Learner; some partners in the UK are E-Learn Design, HowToMoodle, and Remote-Learner UK.

Organization of Moodle

Just like with a wiki, it is important for teaching librarians to keep content organized on a Moodle. Therefore, when using a Moodle to teach a class, a teaching librarian should remember a few guidelines.

- Keep the homepage clean and only provide necessary links on this page, such as links to a syllabus, discussion forum, assignments page...

- Do not put two different types of content on the same page (e.g. do not put a syllabus and a discussion forum on the same page of the Moodle, but place these items on separate pages).

- Do not add pro forma content as the academic term proceeds without giving an adequate explanation as to what the purpose of the content is, giving a concise description of why the content is important, and providing clear links to the content.

- Try to limit the Moodle to as few pages as possible.

- Avoid using too many other Web 2.0 tools in concert with the Moodle, e.g. placing course content on a Moodle and on Facebook, a wiki, a courseware site such as Blackboard, etc. can frustrate a student as he or she has to check multiple online venues to located needed information. Try to use just a Moodle, or a Moodle and one other Web 2.0 tool such as Facebook.

Distinguishing a wiki from a Moodle

So, the question arises, to use or not to use a wiki or a Moodle? As mentioned, both yield benefits and disadvantages, and the following is a juxtaposition of their attributes. Moodles are completely open source, so academies or instructors who implement them have access to all available features and do not have to pay an upgrade fee. Many wikis, however, are commercially owned, e.g. PB Works and Wikispaces, and to access all features academies or instructors may have to pay monthly fees. Moodles tend to have the capacity to support more students. For example, an academy could technically download the Moodle platform and offer all its online courses from this site, whereas wikis do not always have that much capacity. When using a wiki it is better for each librarian to download access, because wiki providers usually offer a limited number of pages (e.g. 20–100) per access. Both learning platforms allow storage space for audio and audio-visual files, links to other websites, and other multimedia. Thus the following suggestions are listed when determining whether to use a Moodle or a wiki.

- For an academy looking to provide a consistent free online learning environment for its faculty and students, a Moodle may be a better choice.
- For an academy encouraging its librarians to choose their own online platform to use during pedagogy, instructors may opt for a Moodle or a wiki.

- For an academy or instructor aiming to ensure the online learning platform does not contain distracting and unattractive advertisements, a Moodle offers an ad-free feature for free, or the instructor may use most wiki platforms and pay a monthly fee to have the ads removed.
- Wikis tend to offer one set format for educators, whereas Moodles offer varied formats such as weekly, topics, social, and SCORM.

When using either a wiki or a Moodle, also remain cognizant of these points.

- A wiki or a Moodle must be organized efficiently or students and librarians will become frustrated and student learning will become obsolete.
- To keep a wiki or Moodle organized offer access to all pages via the course homepage.
- Place different subject-related content on separate pages (e.g. insert the course calendar on one page titled "course calendar"; place the student discussion venue on a separate page titled "student discussion forum"...). Do not place these different content types on the same page.
- As an instructor, monitor the wiki or Moodle daily for inappropriate content, mistakes, student questions, possible plagiarism, copyright infringement...
- As an instructor, communicate to students what is appropriate to post to the wiki or Moodle and what content is not appropriate.
- Catalyze student involvement by posting questions, telling them to view important dates on the calendar, or asking them to post links to websites pertinent to current assignments.
- Deduct points for inappropriate postings to specific wiki pages, such as overly informal content or plagiarism...

- Give students instruction as to what would and would not violate copyright and plagiarism, what is appropriate interaction regarding privacy online, and what is and is not appropriate formal and informal interaction on a class wiki or Moodle.

- Attempt to use only one extra Web 2.0 tool at most alongside either a wiki or a Moodle.

Second Life

Second Life (*http://secondlife.com/*) is a Web 2.0 tool created by Linden Lab that depicts an online virtual world. In this virtual world each user creates and designs his or her own avatar. Obtaining a user name, password, and initial entrance into Second Life (SL) is free. Once inside Second Life, one may use one's avatar to roam about freely and discover various virtual venues created by others. However, some virtual venues require permissions, such as passwords to enter; thus some areas in Second Life are off limits to one's avatar unless it receives a password from the creator of the venue. In any virtual, digital venue to which an avatar has access, the avatar may socialize, perform group projects, develop and barter virtual property and services with other avatars, and build digital virtual venues. An avatar may purchase almost anything in Second Life that he or she could buy in the real world – property, clothes, art, automobiles... One purchases these products with Linden dollars (L$), which is the Second Life currency. An avatar may earn L$ by developing goods and selling them in Second Life, or by obtaining a virtual job in Second Life, such as becoming a model or a performer.

Empirical studies regarding Second Life

Various instructors are beginning to utilize Second Life in their pedagogical endeavors. Empirical research suggests it is another Web 2.0 tool that may enhance student learning. For example, Craig[26] and Dede et al.[27] discovered that using SL encouraged interaction, collaboration, and sharing resources; dissolved social boundaries; and fostered exploration, synthesis, and interaction within a media-rich environment. All these actions encourage the highest level of learning, which is synthesis, according to Bloom's taxonomy.[28] In another empirical study, a graduate seminar in interdisciplinary communication at the University of Texas in Austin implemented Second Life.[29] During this course the students collaborated with architecture students at the university to create sustainable urban housing designs in Second Life. The results of this study suggested the use of Second Life increased student engagement and learning, fostered creative research ideas, and proffered rich-text learning venues.

Other pedagogical endeavors using SL suggested that it improved student learning. For example, the University of Leicester developed the Media Zoo to host archeological classes where students searched for and located archeological findings; offered various academic workshops; and presented training programs to students regarding how to use SL effectively. Each of these uses produced increased student learning.[30]

Example assignment using Second Life

Teaching librarians may create these same positive learning environments with SL in multiple substantive areas. For example, a librarian teaching an aspect of the law could assign students to create a mock courtroom in Second Life, draft a transcript for a mock trial and act it out in Second Life, and then offer peer and teaching librarian review on the positives and negatives of such a presentation. A librarian instructing business students could require them to build a fast-food restaurant in Second Life, create a strategic plan for this restaurant, hire staff, contract with a vendor in Second Life, then attempt to sell food, manage employees... and carry out the strategic plan throughout the semester. Or librarians working with music students could have them create a music hall and then have symphonies, musicals, and other theatrical performances in the hall, manage ticket sales, and create appropriate seating space. Research suggests implementing such assignments in Second Life allows students to partake in active learning in a realistic, real-world context.[31]

Using Adobe Connect

Adobe Connect (*www.adobe.com/products/adobeconnect. html*) is an effective Web 2.0 tool to use as a supplement to another Web 2.0 tool such as a wiki or Moodle. Adobe Connect offers affordable payment options, and only requires an easily uploaded add-on to commence usage. It provides a synchronous venue in which students and instructor may meet at a specified time. Carlson empirically tested Adobe Connect as it was implemented in a bachelor's in science of nursing program at the University of Arizona in the United States,[32] and found it offered many advantages, such as a convenient place for the class and instructor to meet synchronously to discuss a topic, concerns, questions, or upcoming assignments. Adobe Connect also has a webcam view and audio so students may see and hear the instructor as he or she speaks, and see and hear other students. It allows the instructor to open and show students a PowerPoint, graphs, charts, images, animated presentations, or PDFs. Adobe Connect is portable across many mobile devices, such as Android, iPhone, iPad, Playbook, and BlackBerry.

Adobe Connect provides private meeting rooms in which students may create documents, presentations, or other information and store these for future additions. Users can set up their own persistent URLs for private meeting spaces; thus as groups of students are presenting, synchronous meeting areas may be set up that only students may view and not the audience to which they are presenting. Adobe Connect offers rich pods with which students may enhance presentations by sharing video, notes, and files, conduct instant polls, use multiple breakout rooms with private VoIP or telephone conference call, record notes, and use virtual whiteboards.[33] The software allows users to record and archive meetings or presentations. Archived sessions may be referred to by students or teaching librarians later in the academic term, or used by the librarian in subsequent terms provided copyright permission is granted by the student creator. Adobe Connect also offers virtual tools that estimate how engaged a class is, thus teachers may gauge student progress and participation.

Implementing the advantages of Adobe Connect

The advantageous features of this Web 2.0 tool can be utilized in various substantive areas to teach high school, undergraduate, or graduate-level students. For example, graduate students studying clinical psychology in an online format could be given a fictitious case file and asked to submit a video via Adobe Connect acting out how they would consult with and treat the patient; they convey a proposed treatment plan in a PowerPoint, and then meet with their classmates and instructor to present and discuss their creations. The process of creating their own video with a group of peers requires the students to interact via Adobe Connect and implement metacognition by thinking about what they are doing. In other words, they are guided to work with other students in understanding and agreeing upon what diagnosis to give the fictitious patient. Acting out a brief consultation enables students to practice clinician skills and think about the cardinal elements of what constitutes a correct diagnosis, such as a form of depression, post-traumatic stress, or some other illness.

Student use of Adobe Connect to augment presentations

Students can use some of the unique features on Adobe Connect to present their findings. For example, they can utilize this tool's ability to show audio-video and PowerPoints, and use the private meeting spaces to commence a project, save their work, and return to this private space later. Additionally, they can utilize private meeting areas during their presentation to make adjustments without distracting the instructor or other students. The teaching librarian can use these tools to view student engagement of the audience, control who communicates during the presentation, and interject his or her own related video and audio as he or she deems necessary.

Mind maps

Mindomo (*www.mindomo.com/*) is a digital mind-mapping tool a librarian may use when introducing students to new or foreign concepts. Using Mindomo encourages students to convey their thoughts about a new concept or unfamiliar task in a digital format, and also inspires metacognitive thinking – the process of thinking about or critiquing the concepts or ideas about which one is thinking. So if students are working on a project that requires the organization of various elements to make specific chemical compounds, Mindomo can enable them to communicate, organize, and question their thoughts about which elements need to be placed where to form correct compounds. For example, students may be asked to design a digital model of the elements making up sodium bicarbonate. A helpful way to begin this pedagogical task is to use Mindomo to create a digital model of the elements that the student believes make up the compound. Thus a student may think sodium bicarbonate incorporates carbon, hydrogen, oxygen, and sodium. He or she then creates a Mindomo representation of how each of these elements, and how much of each, is arranged within this compound. Then, by examining the model created, he or she is forced to consider critically whether it accurately depicts the sodium bicarbonate compound. Simply picturing the chemical model in one's head may result in error. However, creating a tangible digital picture fosters metacognitive thought, which can help determine whether the model is correctly depicting chemical compounds.

Once students have created a Mindomo map they can print it off to view on paper, thus each mind map developed via Mindomo may be later annotated and critiqued on digital devices or using pen and paper. While annotating, the student may question the elements he or she selected and perform further research. If a student is unsuccessfully attempting to determine which elements make up a compound, he or she may refer back to the Mindomo to help discover where he or she is missing or skipping a step in the process of solving the dilemma. Mindomo representations thus nurture students' ability to critique multiple solutions to a problem or numerous ways of putting a logical puzzle together, instead of just focusing on one. Such promotion of metacognition, multiple thought processes, and self-critique fosters higher-level rich-text thinking, which is the goal of pedagogy. This digital Mindomo-generated model may also be distributed to other students for peer review, disseminated to the instructor for analysis, or used for further private metacognition by the student.

Cost

Mindomo offers users three free maps to test the product; those wishing to create more mind maps must pay for that access. For example, one may have access to creating an unlimited number of mind maps for US$6 (£3.70) a month for six months, or sign up for team access for $9 (£5.60) a month for six months. Some of the features listed on the Mindomo website that come with these fees include:

- advanced exporting and importing
- Mindomo desktop
- embedding videos and audio files
- authenticated task information
- secure connections
- 350MB of storage space.

Empirical research supporting the use of mind maps

Empirical research has illustrated the pedagogical benefits of using mind maps. Dhindsa et al.[34] compared the pedagogical effects and the richness of students' education by offering instruction using mind maps, and identical traditional instruction without the use of mind maps. Their results suggested that the students who utilized mind maps obtained more extensive cognitive structures, exhibited more organized thoughts, and demonstrated richer interconnectedness of thoughts than did the students who received traditional instruction without mind maps.

Other empirical research also found that mind maps produce pedagogical benefits. Issam and Fouad[35] compared an experimental group of 31 eighth-grade students receiving science instruction who were permitted to incorporate the use of mind maps, and a control group of 31 eighth-grade students who were not allowed to use mind maps to understand the science concepts they were being taught. Their results suggested, on average, students in the experimental group who were permitted to use mind maps scored higher on multiple-choice tests measuring the scientific concepts presented than did the students in the control group who were forbidden from utilizing mind maps.

Using Camtasia as a supplement to other Web 2.0 tools

Camtasia (*www.techsmith.com/camtasia.html*) is another effective Web 2.0 tool that may be used in concert with a wiki, Moodle, or Mindomo. Using Camtasia, one may record any type of media for later usage, such as audio, audio-visual, or a combination of a PowerPoint with audio. After producing a recording, an instructor or student may save such a production, archive it, and use it when convenient and appropriate. Other benefits offered by Camtasia include being able to watch a lecture file for review before an exam, and having access to the file to discuss substantive issues with peers. Further, after pre-recording a lecture, it may be conveniently tweaked by the instructor for subsequent academic terms, thus saving valuable time. Other benefits include the following.

- It is easy to edit any recording.
- It offers a media-assist library from which one may add banners, videos, and various backgrounds.
- It proffers the ability to add creative visual effects to one's presentations.
- It promotes efficiency in splicing together still screens, audio, and video.

- It is portable across media (PCs, laptops, iPhone, iPad…).

- It provides valuable flexibility for students.

- It saves librarians time and is easy to use.

- Content placed on Camtasia is easy to preserve, store, and tweak for future use in subsequent academic terms (but be cognizant that future use of students' tangible creations requires copyright permission from those students, fair-use exceptions, or section 108 of Title 17 exceptions).

- It offers students access to vital information 24/7.

- It allows easy transferability so one may quickly and efficiently share videos with colleagues.

YouTube

YouTube (*www.youtube.com/*) is a dynamic Web 2.0 tool with which many students are familiar, and librarians can use it to engage students better. A 2012 Nielsen poll indicated the majority of teenagers now access their music via YouTube rather than by listening to the radio, purchasing MP3s, or buying CDs. This poll, published in *The Guardian*, indicated that two-thirds of teenagers access and use YouTube, 64 percent of teenagers stated they use YouTube to obtain their music, 56 percent listened to the radio, 53 percent access and listen to music via iTunes, and 50 percent listen to CDs.[36] With this knowledge, teaching librarians are wise to utilize YouTube in their pedagogy. Empirical research has proved that individuals learn new content by making connections with this content via well-established knowledge or with venues in which one is quite comfortable. Thus by implementing YouTube in their work, teaching librarians are fostering ease of learning for students tackling new curricula.

Many instructors are cognizant of the profound impact YouTube has on individuals aged 30 and younger, and have begun using it in their pedagogy. For example, one instructor notes that allowing students to post links to YouTube catalyzes discussion in class. Recently a student in this instructor's class posted a link to a YouTube clip of Alanis Morisette's parody of a Black Eyed Peas' song. This ignited a spirited discussion regarding how women's sexuality is utilized in popular culture. Further, a field study in an after-school program with middle school students discovered that by employing YouTube in their pedagogy, this Web 2.0 tool elicited an emotional response in the students: they formed a cognitive connection to it, and thus increased their level of engagement with the curriculum.[37] The author further advocated that when using YouTube in formal or informal pedagogy, an instructor should encourage students not to be passive receivers of the content, but rather learn to be critical of what they are viewing.

Potential copyright problem with YouTube

In the United States and the United Kingdom, if someone links to a website that contains infringing content, the person who created the links may be deemed to have committed indirect copyright infringement. Thus if a teaching librarian wants to link to websites, or wants students to link to content for a class assignment, it is best to link to the site's homepage. By doing so, any infringing material contained in deep links is not directly linked to your or your students' websites. Then simply orally tell students that they may want to look at other content on a website that is obtained by investigating deeper into the site. But do not link, or encourage students to link, to deep websites; only link to a website's homepage, to avoid possible association with copyright infringement.[38]

This distinction is important: just because clips of music, speeches, cartoons, and other forms of entertainment state they are in compliance with UK, US, or other versions of copyright does not mean they are. For example, a music video posted on YouTube may provide great pedagogical content to discuss in a literature, religion, women's issues, law, or music class. However, if a student or a librarian is linking directly to this video and it has been posted without copyright permission, this may be considered copyright infringement in the United Kingdom and the United States. As a result, the librarian hosting the class, the sponsoring university, and the student could be sued for copyright infringement. To help prevent such unintended infringement and encourage students not to link directly to a video, simply have students link to the YouTube homepage. Then if a librarian or student wants the rest of the class to view a particular video, instruct them to perform a keyword search on the homepage to find the video. This technique prevents possible copyright violation by linking to the YouTube homepage rather than a deep link within the site.

Example assignment using YouTube

Librarians may utilize YouTube when giving instruction in a number of substantive areas. For example, librarians giving bibliographic instruction regarding music can use YouTube by playing short clips of various contemporary songs and then showing students how to cite this music, or a book, article, or speech about the songs. Just ensure the clips you are showing are copyright compliant. By including modern, popular music in pedagogy, the librarian has captured the students' interest and given the pupils a familiar academic anchor from which to make connections to new content, such as bibliographic citation. Teaching librarians could further embrace YouTube in their curricula when discussing how to use an electronic database. For example, a librarian wanting to demonstrate using specific electronic databases to locate certain information can record a live tutorial with screenshots displaying how to locate articles in EBSCO Academic Search Complete, and load this video to YouTube. By providing a link to the video, students may access it later in the semester when completing a term paper or project requiring the use of electronic databases. Such a tool gives students a familiar medium on which to learn (64 percent of teenagers stated they use YouTube[39]), and such familiarity facilitates learning.

Ergo, here is a list of points to consider when using YouTube in one's pedagogy.

- Remember, most teenagers now use YouTube to obtain their music. These teenagers (now in junior high or high school) will soon be the majority of students in college and graduate school.

- Encourage criticism and metacognition in students as they view content on YouTube, and try to prevent passive indulgence.

- Be cautious of allowing students to post YouTube videos to class discussion boards, distance-learning sites, class webpages… Such posting directly to a music video or other performance may result in unintended copyright infringement.

- Instead, post links to YouTube's homepage and then perform keyword searches to locate music. Encourage students to do the same.

- Do not assume a music video, speech, cartoon, or other content on YouTube is copyright compliant just because it is marked in that manner. Do your homework, and link to the YouTube homepage.

- Remember, the use of YouTube and other Web 2.0 tools in pedagogy fosters connections for students between familiar content and the new curriculum they are attempting to learn. These connections result in more student engagement with the academic content and a richer learning environment that stimulates the visual, auditory, and tactile senses, and may also elicit an emotional response that can enhance student learning.

Choosing a pertinent Web 2.0 tool

Based on the information garnered from the above-mentioned empirical studies, teaching librarians first need to decide on a specific Web 2.0 tool that meets their pedagogical needs. For example, law librarians may choose to use a wiki in their classroom because this digital tool can be used to have students draft bills, proposed regulations, mock trial scripts, pleadings, or other legal documents. A wiki forum provides an excellent venue in which students can asynchronously collaborate, disagree with one another, and edit documents. Supplementing a wiki with Facebook, Google+, or some other informal venue benefits students and the educator in that they may use this asynchronous platform to discuss where to meet to draft a bill on the wiki, ask the teaching librarian questions and receive answers, or chat informally to relieve stress. By using these two Web 2.0 tools synchronously, the students are provided with a formal tool to complete assignments and an informal tool to chat, ask queries, plan meetings, and conduct other administrative endeavors. However, a teaching librarian needs to select a Web 2.0 tool that meets students' targeted needs.

- Mindomo fosters mental connections from familiar content to new and unknown information, and encourages metacognition. For example, pre-medical students creating Mindomo maps may better understand which pathogens cause specific diseases by mapping known causes and pathogens to possible correlated pathogens.

- Second Life assists architectural students in envisioning three-dimensional models of potential structures.

- YouTube provides familiar, entertaining venues for students to make connections to new not-so-entertaining information. Such entertainment stimulation can get students' synapses firing and enable them to think critically and promote better inculcation of information.

- Facebook offers an informal venue for students to joke, vent, and discuss related substantive content. Discussion of informal content is not to be discounted as it may still lead to students learning formal class content.

- Camtasia is a good distance-learning tool with which to discuss issues, and record and archive lectures.

Again it should be stressed that, while tempting, a teaching librarian should avoid trying to implement more than two of these tools per academic term. Forcing students to obtain content from or add it to more than two venues during a semester can generate stress and frustration. Some pedagogical scenarios may even mandate only using one of these Web 2.0 tools, especially if a face-to-face class component is utilized as well.

Meeting the needs of non-traditional students

Teaching librarians must remain cognizant of the variety of students that currently attend college or graduate school. Each Web 2.0 tool selected should be adequate to promote learning in all types of students. For example, for reasons such as personal desire to find a more mentally challenging job, losing a job due to cyclical economic hardship, the desire to increase one's job skills, or simply wanting a new hobby, numerous individuals are returning to school later in life. Hence librarians will serve as a guide to 18–24-year-olds, people at mid-life, and elderly students as well. Further, many of these individuals who return to school may have some form of physical or mental disability. Yet universities that have developed an online learning model present learning opportunities to these non-traditional learners that were not available and convenient ten years ago. When selecting an online tool to improve the educational environment and create a rich-text learning experience, it is important to keep three variables in mind.

- *Improve communication*. Whichever tool is selected, it should improve communication between student and instructor, and between student and student. It should offer a rich-text environment by stimulating as many senses as possible: visual, auditory, and kinesthetic. The Web 2.0 tool selected should promote these benefits for all students regardless of their age, presence of a disability, sex, race, or learning style.

- *Provide equal access*. Usability features should promote learning for all regardless of their age, disability, or experience with computers.

- *Foster efficiency*. Offer features that foster efficient means of exchanging and crafting documents and ideas.

Conclusion

In conclusion, today's student, regardless of whether she is 18 or 99, wants to be led by an academic guide, desires flexible course content, and does not want to be given strict pedagogical boundaries. Using Web 2.0 tools such as Facebook, Google+, Camtasia, wikis, Second Life, and others in the classroom provides such flexibility and challenges for all students. Teaching librarians should select a couple of these Web 2.0 tools, master their functionalities, and then offer them to students in an organized fashion. Further, teaching librarians should provide these tools in a manner that proffers equal access, quality, and effective communication, and ultimately fosters metacognition, which leads to high-level learning and synthesis of new knowledge.

Notes

1. Cifuentes, L., Xochihua, O.A., and Edwards, J.C. (2011) 'Learning in Web 2.0 environments: surface learning and chaos or deep learning and self-regulation?', *Quarterly Review of Distance Education*, 12(1): 1–21.
2. Stark-Wroblewski, K., Kreiner, D.S., Boeding, C.M., Lopata, A.N., Ryan, J.J., and Church, T.M. (2008) 'Use of virtual reality technology to enhance undergraduate learning in abnormal psychology', *Teaching of Psychology*, 35(4): 343–8.
3. Cifuentes et al., note 1 above.
4. Veeravagu, J., Muthusamy, C., Marimuthu, R., and Subrayan, A. (2010) 'Using Bloom's taxonomy to gauge students' reading comprehension performance', *Canadian Social Science*, 6(3): 205–12.
5. Kim, M., Patel, R.A., Uchizono, J.A., and Beck, L. (2012) 'Incorporation of Bloom's taxonomy into multiple-choice examination questions for a pharmacotherapeutics course', *American Journal of Pharmaceutical Education*, 76(6): 1–8.
6. Hay, D.B. (2007) 'Using concept maps to measure deep, surface and non-learning outcomes', *Studies in Higher Education*, 32(1): 39–57.

7. Connolly, M., Jones, C., and Jones, N. (2007) 'New approaches, new vision: capturing teacher experiences in a brave new online world', *Open Learning*, 22(1): 43–56.
8. Davis, F.F. and Loasby, I.D. (2009) 'I love legal history: Web 2.0 and the teaching of law', *Journal of Commonwealth Law and Legal Education*, 7(1): 19–36.
9. Veeravagu et al., note 4 above.
10. Davis and Loasby, note 8 above.
11. Varga-Atkins, T., Dangerfield, P., and Brigden, D. (2010) 'Developing professionalism through the use of wikis: a study with first-year undergraduate medical students', *Medical Teacher*, 32: 824–9.
12. Zhang, X. and Olfman, L. (2010) 'Studios, mini-lectures, project presentations, class blog and wiki: a new approach to teaching web technologies', *Journal of Information Technology Education: Innovations in Practice*, 9: 187–99.
13. Sherman, M. (1971) 'Environment and learning', *Education*, 91(4): 277–80.
14. Cooper, J. (1979) 'Actions really do speak louder than words', *Nursing*, 9(4): 113–18.
15. Zhang and Olfman, note 12 above.
16. Rick, J., Guzdial, M., and Carroll, K. (2002) 'Collaborative learning at low cost: CoWeb use in English composition', paper presented at Computer Support for Collaborative Learning Conference, 7–11 January, Boulder, CO; available at: *http://citeseerx.ist.psu.edu/viewdoc/summary?* (accessed: 26 February 2013), p. 1.
17. Noveck, B.S. (2007) 'Wikipedia and the future of legal education', *Journal of Legal Education*, 57(1): 3–9.
18. Achterman, D. (2008) 'Making connections with blogs and wikis', *California School Library Association Journal*, 30(1): 29–30.
19. Stark-Wroblewski et al., note 2 above.
20. Md Ali, N. and Jaafar, J.M. (2010) 'Transforming Moodle as a reflective tool in learning French language', *International Journal of Academic Research*, 2(3): 238–40.
21. Henninger, M. and Kutter, A.K. (2010) 'Integration of education and technology – a long term study about possibilities

and adequacy of a learning management system for education', *Systemics, Cybernetics and Informatics*, 8(3): 10–14.

22. Md Ali and Jaafar, note 20 above.

23. Ibid.

24. Moodle, 'Language packs'; available at: *http://docs.moodle.org/23/en/Language_packs* (accessed: 22 February 2013).

25. Moodle, 'Course formats'; available at: *http://docs.moodle.org/22/en/Course_formats* (accessed: 22 February 2013).

26. Craig, E. (2007) 'Meta-perspectives on the metaverse: a blogosphere debate on the significance of Second Life', paper presented at ED-MEDIA World Conference on Educational Multimedia, Hypermedia & Telecommunications, 25 June, Vancouver.

27. Dede, C., Clark, J., Ketelhut, D., Nelson, B., and Bowman, C. (2005) 'Fostering motivation, learning, and transfer in multi-user virtual environments', paper presented at American Educational Research Associating Conference, 11–15 April, Montreal.

28. Lord, T. and Baviskar, S. (2007) 'Moving students from information recitation to information understanding: exploiting Bloom's taxonomy in creating science questions', *Journal of College Science Teaching*, 36(5): 40–4.

29. Jarmon, L., Traphagan, T., and Mayrath, M. (2008) 'Understanding project-based learning in Second Life with a pedagogy, training, and assessment trio', *Educational Media International*, 45(3): 157–76.

30. Wheeler, M. (2009) 'Developing the Media Zoo in Second Life', *British Journal of Educational Technology*, 40(3): 427–43.

31. Raymond, P. (2010) 'Virtual worlds and social networking: reaching the millennials', *Journal of Technology Research*, 2(1): 1–15.

32. Carlson, K. (2012) 'Using Adobe Connect to deliver online library instruction to the RN to BSN program', *Journal of Library & Information Services in Distance Learning*, 5(4): 172–80.

33. Harvel, G. and Hardmann, W. (2012) 'A comparison of different communications tools for distance learning in nuclear education', *Journal of Energy and Power Engineering*, 6: 20–33.

34. Dhindsa, H.S., Kasim, M., and Anderson, O.R. (2011) 'Constructivist-visual mind map teaching approach and the quality of students' cognitive structures', *Journal of Science Educational Technology*, 20: 186–200.

35. Issam, A. and Fouad, A. (2008) 'The influence of mind mapping on eighth graders' science achievement', *School Science & Mathematics*, 108(7): 298–312.

36. Michaels, S. (2012) 'YouTube is teens' first choice for music', *The Guardian*, 16 August; available at: *www.guardian.co.uk/music/2012/aug/16/youtube-teens-first-choice-music* (accessed: 15 February 2013).

37. Walker, J. (2008) 'Examining the intersections of popular culture & youth radio after-school', *Youth Media Reporter*, 2(1/6): 201–20.

38. Hoffmann, G.M. (2005) *Copyright in Cyberspace 2*. London: Neal-Schuman Publishers.

39. Michaels, note 36 above.

2

Using the LibGuides platform for more than just hosting electronic pathfinders

Abstract: This chapter provides an overview of the LibGuides platform, its Web 2.0 features, its support and training services, and its relevancy in librarianship. The chapter describes best practices and pedagogical uses of LibGuides specifically and subject guides generally for teaching librarians. It also examines the use of LibGuides at specific institutions, and explores research into student use and perception of the platform. It discusses considerations teaching librarians need to be aware of prior to purchasing and implementing the platform at their institutions.

Key words: pathfinders, Web 2.0, LibGuides, subject guides, course guides, information literacy, distance learning, chat reference.

Introduction

LibGuides (*http://springshare.com/libguides/*) is an online platform that allows libraries to create and maintain electronic pathfinders and other materials utilizing many Web 2.0 applications. It is currently being used at more than 3,700 academic, public, special, and school libraries worldwide.[1] Librarians can customize their guides and

LibGuides site to create a uniform aesthetic, or create a variety of guides using various themes. Some librarians use the platform simply to create and house electronic versions of their print research guides or pathfinders. Others use it as their library website, or to promote library services and events. There are also many pedagogical uses of LibGuides, such as providing library and research instruction, homework assistance, and information literacy tools. Teaching librarians can create subject or course-specific guides to direct students and faculty to the most useful databases and other library materials in that area.[2]

While LibGuides offers many useful features and benefits to teaching librarians, it does so at a price. Depending on the size of the institution, the platform can be very expensive to implement. Librarians who are unfamiliar with Web 2.0 applications may find it difficult to learn to use. Some have difficulty getting patrons to find and use the materials they post on their LibGuides platform. Teaching librarians need to market the platform heavily to ensure patrons not only find but also use and explore the guides created at their institutions.

Web 2.0 features and support in the LibGuides platform

The LibGuides platform offers a range of Web 2.0 features that can be easily added to guides.[3] The platform is tablet friendly, has mobile site capabilities, and allows teaching librarians to interact with patrons via social networking sites like Facebook and Twitter. Patrons can be informed when new guides are published in certain subjects or a particular guide has been updated by subscribing to email alerts and RSS

(Rich Site Summary) feeds. Teaching librarians can make guides interactive by allowing patrons to submit links to guides, inserting interactive polls, or utilizing LibChat, a feature that allows patrons conducting research to chat with a librarian. Teaching librarians can also add information from outside sources by embedding media or podcasts and inserting active links to other websites. The LibGuides platform has a built-in link checker that alerts librarians to any broken links in guides so these can be fixed. The platform also gives teaching librarians the option to include Google Scholar, web, book, or patent search boxes in guides. Librarians can include a list of all available electronic databases and allow patrons to search the library's catalog directly from the LibGuides platform.

In addition to the many Web 2.0 features listed above, the LibGuides platform offers extensive support and training to its users. Librarians can create trial accounts to test out the platform prior to purchasing and implementing it at their institutions. Those who sign up for a trial account can access all features and test out the administrative functions as well. There is an extensive help site[4] that introduces users to the platform and walks them through the basics of setting up their LibGuides account and adding collaborators (librarians who create the guides). Users can also find information on this site to customize[5] their LibGuides platforms. Administrators can decide whether the guides at their institutions will follow a pre-set theme, with every guide using the same colors, fonts, and box types, or whether to leave those choices up to the individual guide authors. The help site includes information on best practices and has links to its community[6] and 'best of'[7] sites. The community site allows users to search every public guide available on the LibGuides platform, has forums for librarians to share thoughts and ideas, and hosts the LibGuides blog and Twitter feed. The 'best of' site houses excellent examples of guides from libraries around the world. Users can review these to get ideas for their own guides, use excerpts, or copy the guides completely to post on their LibGuides sites. The help site also includes a mobile site builder,[8] which allows librarians to create a library site that their patrons can easily access and use on their mobile devices. Finally, the help site has a link to the training schedule,[9] where users can sign up for free webinars on various topics throughout the year.

The platform provides several tools[10] for librarians to monitor usage of their guides. The system summary report provides information on a library's LibGuides site in general, such as how many guides have been created, how many collaborators there are, how many times the platform has been accessed, and how many Web 2.0 features like embedded content, podcasts, and links have been included in guides. Librarians can also run reports on individual guides to see how many times they have been viewed, which links patrons clicked on, and whether the guides were viewed on the standard or mobile site.

Relevance and use of the LibGuides platform: a study

In 2011 Ghaphery and White[11] conducted research on how libraries use electronic research guides generally. In their study, the authors compiled data from 99 university libraries' electronic guides and also conducted a separate survey of 198 librarians throughout the United States who create and use such guides. They found that a majority of the libraries studied use the LibGuides platform. Among the 99 libraries studied, 63 use LibGuides, and 129 of the 198 survey respondents use this platform to host and maintain their electronic guides. A majority of the survey respondents indicated that they also use the LibGuides platform to host course pages and instruction on the use of library resources. Forty percent of those surveyed include an alphabetical list of all library databases on their LibGuides site, while 31 percent include library information such as hours, directions, and staff listings. Ghaphery and White also found that some libraries instituted policies for use and maintenance of the guides on the platform. A majority of those surveyed indicated they have policies in place for the maintenance of guides, as well as style guidelines to ensure uniformity among the guides created at their institutions. Often links to outside sources are included in guides, and 46 percent of librarians surveyed stated that they have policies in place to check periodically that these links are still correct. Many of those surveyed indicated that they require certain information like pictures, contacts, operating information, etc., to be included in each guide. Some librarians even require training on the platform to be provided to guide creators.

Ghaphery and White also asked whether librarians evaluate their guides, and if so, how. About 23 percent of the respondents had no evaluation tools in place, while around 20 percent measured user statistics in their evaluations. The authors concluded that electronic research guides are now very common and a large number of libraries have selected the LibGuides platform to host their electronic guides.

This study indicates that LibGuides is heavily used in libraries throughout the United States. It also points out a need for librarians to create and adhere to policies on the use and maintenance of the platform. Teaching librarians should consider crafting policies to confirm that the content in their guides is up to date, links are functioning properly, and any style guidelines are followed by all librarian collaborators at an institution. Librarians may also want to implement an evaluation method to ensure that their intended audience is utilizing the guides.

Uses for teaching librarians – at the reference desk and beyond

Librarians are constantly engaged in teaching, whether in the form of formal pedagogy in the classroom or informal instruction at the reference desk. Teaching librarians can utilize LibGuides in many ways to improve their teaching and foster patron learning. The following are examples of ways librarians can incorporate subject guides on the LibGuides platform in the course of their work.

One of the easiest ways to incorporate the LibGuides platform into informal instruction is to create subject guides that answer recurring patron questions. These guides are especially useful during library orientation sessions, and for answering questions at the reference desk. When a patron has a subject-specific question, the librarian on duty can direct him or her to the relevant guide on the topic. These subject guides should include links to items in the library's catalog, information on and links to relevant databases and electronic resources available, and links to outside sources as well. The guides should also contain information on basic research methods and where to go or who to contact for additional assistance. Librarians should consider creating guides that provide instruction on how to use certain features of the library. For example, guides can be created on how to search for materials using the library's catalog or electronic resources. These instructional guides can include embedded video tutorials created by librarians to illustrate how to use various resources. All guides created on the LibGuides platform include printer-friendly versions, so it may be useful to print out copies to have available at the reference desk. Patrons can then refer back to the guides and use them without having to access the internet.

Teaching librarians can also use the guides created using LibGuides to provide distance reference. These days, much reference and instruction is provided via phone, email, and chat. Instead of trying to explain how to find a certain resource or how to conduct research in a particular subject, librarians can refer patrons to the appropriate guide. All guides have the option of including LibChat or other instant messaging services, where patrons can talk directly to librarians while using the guides. This allows librarians to answer questions about the specific guide the patron is using and refer the user to related resources.

The subject guides created on LibGuides can be used in conjunction with QR (quick response) codes. Librarians can create QR codes to print and place in various areas in the library, such as in the stacks in different subject areas or at computer terminals. Patrons can then scan the codes with their mobile devices to pull up the related subject or instructional guides. The LibGuides platform is mobile ready, so guides pulled up on a mobile device are reformatted for better viewing. Librarians who prefer not to create QR codes directing patrons to guides can instead print out guides and place them with related subject materials in the stacks.

Another use of the LibGuides platform is to highlight special collections or events at the library or institution. For example, librarians at West Chester University collaborated with faculty to create a guide promoting campus events celebrating Abraham Lincoln's 200th birthday.[12] Any interested patron could go to the guide to find information about library and web resources on Lincoln and the presentations and events on campus related to the celebration. The librarians also created a guide with members of the career development center to highlight information and research resources available at both the library and the career center. Teaching librarians should consider collaborating with faculty and staff in different departments to create guides that cater to patrons' needs both in and out of the library.

In conclusion, teaching librarians who want to include the LibGuides platform in their informal instruction should consider the following.

- Create guides that answer recurring patron questions.

- Subject guides should include links to items in the library's catalog, information on and links to relevant databases and electronic resources, and links to outside sources on the topic. Consider creating and embedding video tutorials on how to conduct research in the subject area and how to use specific databases.

- Create instructional guides on how to use the library's catalog to find materials.

- Refer patrons to guides to facilitate distance reference.

- Create QR codes that direct patrons to relevant guides on the LibGuides platform, or print guides and place with related materials in the stacks.

- Include contact information and/or a chat box so that patrons can get additional research assistance as needed.

- Collaborate with faculty and staff to create guides that highlight special collections, resources, and events.

Uses for teaching librarians – in the classroom

While general library subject guides are great tools to familiarize patrons with library resources and services, course-specific guides may be one of the best uses of the LibGuides platform for teaching librarians. Whether invited to provide bibliographic instruction in another professor's class or teaching a class on her own, course-specific guides allow the teaching librarian to create guides that highlight the most useful resources for the students in the class. Librarians can include information for the specific databases, books, journals, and websites that students will use in their research without oversaturating them with information. Course-specific guides make students aware that such research tools are available to them, and may even get students to browse and use other guides on the library's LibGuides platform. As Reeb and Gibbons[13] stated in their study on student use of subject guides:

> Guides that are organized or delivered at the course level appear to be more in line with how students approach library research. If librarians are to meet students where they are, we need to move away from the traditional use of discipline-based to more course-based devices for organizing library resources.

In other words, guides tailored to specific courses are more appealing to students than general subject guides; thus, students are more likely to use course-specific guides when conducting their research.

Teaching librarians who provide library or bibliographic instruction should try to get faculty members involved in promoting student use of course-specific guides. Librarians should introduce the LibGuides platform to faculty staff and let them know that guides can be created for their individual courses. Librarians should identify the Web 2.0 tools that can be used and point out that these tools encourage active student interaction, which fosters deep-level learning. Features worth highlighting include chat boxes (so students can interact directly with librarians while using the guides), interactive polls, and the ability to embed media from outside sources and links to the library's catalog and electronic resources.

Librarians should also mention that the course guides can be linked to or embedded in online course platforms, such as Blackboard, or used as course websites where all materials for individual courses are located. Additionally, the guides can be used similarly to a Moodle or wiki: students can contribute to the course materials by adding links and content to the guide. Course-specific guides can also be used effectively for distance education[14] or asynchronous learning in place of live instruction by embedding short videos on how to use certain resources or conduct research in a particular subject area. Students can access these videos at any time convenient to them. Teaching librarians and faculty members can have students view videos prior to class to alleviate time restraints and focus on face-to-face experimentation during the live-instruction sessions.

Teaching librarians who create course-specific guides should consider all aspects of a course and the research students will be conducting for that course. For example, the COMM233 guide[15] created by librarian Tiffany Hebb at DePauw University includes examples of reference materials, books, journals, newspapers, websites, RSS feeds, and podcasts that may be helpful to students enrolled in that course. The information presented is uncluttered, easy to access, and simple to follow. Materials available in the library are linked to their catalog records and include call numbers, so students can easily locate them in the library. When creating the guide, Hebb included links to many outside sources and embedded videos dealing with the course subject matter. Students are able to contact the librarian via a chat box, email, or telephone; all contact information is located on the homepage of the guide. Additionally, students can schedule a research appointment with the librarian simply by clicking an appointment box. The librarian's calendar of availability pops up and students can choose a convenient meeting time. All these features help students access research materials related to their course and make obtaining further research assistance as simple as clicking a button.

As another example of effective use of Web 2.0 tools in course-specific guides, Neves and Dooley[16] discuss the guides created on the LibGuides platform for undergraduate medical students at the W.K. Kellogg Health Sciences Library at Dalhousie University in Halifax, Nova Scotia, Canada. These guides contained resources chosen specifically to assist the students in their coursework and clinical rotations. The librarians attempted to include mostly electronic resources, so students could access the materials at any time. The guides were made interactive by including the Meebo instant messaging service: the Meebo widget made it possible for students to get librarian assistance while using the guides. Students were able to contribute content to the guides by submitting links to other resources that they found while conducting research. The librarians at the W.K. Kellogg Health Science Library received mostly positive feedback from the students, and also noted a sharp increase in their use of the guides.

One specific type of teaching in which librarians engage is information literacy – making sure patrons know how to access, analyze, and use information and information resources. Information literacy instruction is especially important at academic libraries (see the Information Literacy Competency Standards for Higher Education created by the Association of College & Research Libraries[17]). Librarians at Bloomsburg University of Pennsylvania used the LibGuides platform to produce an information literacy tutorial for students at the university.[18] The tutorial was created by combining material from a once-offered one-credit 'Introduction to Library Research' course with parts of James Madison University Library's 'Go for the Gold' information literacy tutorial (the 'Go for the Gold' tutorial authors gave permission to the librarians at Bloomsburg to use information and exercises within the tutorial). The librarians also created two assessment tools to test students' understanding of the information provided in the tutorial: one assessment tool was created specifically for faculty to post to their course pages; the other was embedded into the LibGuides tutorial, so that students could assess themselves. Faculty responded favorably to the tutorial, with many expressing interest in using it in their courses in the future.

Librarians at West Chester University also created an information literacy guide on LibGuides.[19] It was designed for faculty at the university and contained pages for instruction and assessment. The librarians included embedded videos and tutorials as well as librarian contact information on their instruction page. Information about information literacy in general as well as tools to assess students were included on the assessment page. The librarians noted that faculty members heavily used the information literacy guide, which was the most-viewed guide on the LibGuides platform at West Chester University.

In conclusion, teaching librarians who want to include the LibGuides platform in their instruction should consider the following.

- If conducting library or bibliographic instruction, work with faculty members to encourage use of course guides. Highlight important features of the guides to faculty, and include information on how to link to or embed guides in their course sites.

- If teaching a course, consider using LibGuides to create a course guide that serves as the course homepage. House all course materials on the guide, such as the syllabus, calendar, and assignments. Be sure to include course-related library materials and resources, and information on how to access them.

- Consider creating and embedding video tutorials on how to conduct research in the subject area and how to use specific databases.

- Share rich information such as videos, audio files, and links to outside sources.

- Make the guides interactive by allowing students to contribute links to helpful resources, websites, or other material. If allowing students to contribute content to the guides, they should be instructed on what is and is not appropriate to post, and what constitutes plagiarism and/ or copyright infringement.

- Include contact information and/or a chat box so that students can get additional research assistance as needed.

Course-specific guides can be a great instruction tool for teaching librarians and an even better research tool for students, but they need to be accessible and organized. More information on best practices for creating guides on the LibGuides platform can be found later in this chapter.

Considerations: cost, time, patron use, and copyright and plagiarism

Cost

As noted previously, while the LibGuides platform offers many useful features and benefits to teaching librarians, it does so at a price. Depending on the size of the institution, a license to LibGuides costs between US$899 and $2,999 (£570–£1,900) per year.[20] The features and utility of the platform may justify the license fee, but to some libraries this cost may be prohibitive. Other considerations that may impact the decision to license and implement LibGuides include the time it takes to set up, maintain, and market the platform, whether patrons actually use the guides, and ensuring that content included is not plagiarized and does not infringe copyright laws.

Time

The use and implementation of LibGuides are a time-consuming endeavor. Accounts must be made for each librarian collaborator. Librarians must decide whether to have a style guide to ensure uniformity among guides across the platform, regardless of which librarians create them. In addition, librarians must consider what other policies they want to draft and implement regarding the use and maintenance of the LibGuides platform. Training on the platform, particularly for less tech-savvy librarians, can take some time. Although use of the Web 2.0 tools in LibGuides is pretty straightforward, librarians who are less familiar with the tools themselves may have difficulty using these features at first. It may be a good idea to have less tech-savvy librarian collaborators view the instructional tutorials available on the LibGuides help site prior to using and creating guides.

Creating guides on LibGuides takes librarians away from their other tasks, so teaching librarians must ensure their intended audience is using the platform, and that the guides themselves are worth the time taken to create and maintain them. Once librarians are comfortable with the platform, the guides are relatively easy to create. This allows teaching librarians to create many guides, which in turn makes more work for librarians in the form of maintenance.[21] Librarians must maintain guides to ensure their students and other patrons continue to receive relevant information that suits their research needs. While the built-in link checker makes sure all included links are not broken, librarians still need to check manually that the links continue to direct patrons to the correct website. If librarians include information about relevant materials like books or library databases, they will need to check that the most recent edition of the book is noted, catalog records to library materials are correct, and the database links are working. Guides covering hot topics and subjects that constantly change, such as law, need to be checked to ensure the information included is current and correct.

Certain Web 2.0 features included in the platform, such as LibChat, require librarians to be available to help patrons who are using the guides. LibChat is a real-time online chat service that allows patrons to ask librarians for assistance while using guides to conduct research.[22] This requires librarians to commit even more of their time to LibGuides and further takes them away from other tasks. Librarians must be available to chat with those using guides that have the LibChat feature, otherwise patrons may rightly complain that this feature should not be included if the librarian is not available at convenient times.

Student use and perception of subject guides

As noted in several studies on the topic, student use and perception of electronic subject and course guides depend heavily on awareness of the guides. Thus teaching librarians need to market the LibGuides platform widely to ensure patron awareness and use. To illustrate this point, in their research article on the subject, McMullin and Hutton[23] mention three guides created by librarians at West Chester University of Pennsylvania and explain that the number of times each guide was accessed by the intended audience (students) during a two-month evaluation period depended on how that guide was or was not promoted. The first guide the authors studied was published without any form of promotion or marketing; it received 44 views during the two-month period. A link to the second guide was sent to faculty members whose students would be interested in the material presented; that guide was viewed 101 times during the two-month period. The final guide was demonstrated in several library instructional sessions for students, and was viewed 742 times in the evaluation period. Other factors may have influenced the number of views each received, but marketing and promotion seemed to play a big role in student use of these particular guides. Fortunately, the LibGuides platform allows quick and easy marketing of guides via social media such as Facebook and Twitter. However, not all patrons will use a library's social networking sites, so more traditional marketing via the library's website, email, display cases, newsletters, and/or word of mouth may be needed.

Several studies have shown that students who have attended library instruction sessions that highlight subject guides or the LibGuides platform are more likely to return to both the specific guide highlighted and the LibGuides platform in general.[24] In her case study of student use of subject guides at San Jose State University, Staley surveyed 1,031 students from three distinct disciplines: nursing, journalism and mass communications, and organization and management.[25] Students from all three disciplines indicated that they used the Articles & Databases page in their respective subject guides more than any other page. Of those surveyed, nearly half the respondents who indicated that they received library instruction noted they accessed the Articles & Databases page at least five times over the period of a year; whereas only about 16 percent of respondents who did not receive library instruction accessed the Articles & Databases page five or more times during the year. Additionally, only one-quarter of those who did not receive library instruction accessed the homepage of the subject guide, compared to over half of those who did receive library instruction. Overall, most respondents indicated that the subject guides were useful, whether or not they received library instruction or accessed the guides on a regular basis.

In a different study conducted at the University of Alberta and Grant MacEwan University, 11 students participated in interviews designed to ascertain their perceptions and use of subject guides on the LibGuides platform.[26] Ouellette set out to determine how students use these guides and what they like and dislike about them. Participants discussed actual research assignments they undertook and how they found information to complete these, whether they had used subject guides on the LibGuides platform prior to the interview, what features of the guides they considered to be useful, and what features they deemed unhelpful. Most of the respondents in this study indicated that they did not use the subject guides. Many did not know they existed, others preferred to conduct research using Google or other internet resources, and some did not find the guides useful. The students indicated that they would use subject guides as a last resort in their research process or if their instructors suggested such use. Most respondents who had used subject guides prior to the interview indicated they used them mainly to locate databases in their field of study. In terms of what students liked and disliked, most respondents noted that the guides contained too much information, which made using them difficult. Respondents also indicated inconsistency among guides across the LibGuides platform as something they disliked. Similar tabs were labeled differently on various guides, which caused confusion for respondents. Additionally, most students did not like the layout of the guides.

While this study surveyed the perceptions of a very small number of students, it does provide insight into how teaching librarians can improve subject guides so that students not only use but also enjoy using them. It goes to reason that the more students are aware of LibGuides and have positive perceptions of the guides on the platform, the more often the guides will be used.

Copyright and plagiarism

Teaching librarians must be mindful of plagiarism and copyright implications when creating guides on their LibGuides platform. Any material not created by the librarian collaborator must have proper citation to the original work. In some cases, proper citation alone is not enough to prevent claims of copyright infringement. If a teaching librarian assigns creation of guides to students, the librarian must get copyright permission from those students for any future use of the guides on the LibGuides platform.

The teaching librarian should also instruct students on proper citation techniques for a variety of formats to avoid plagiarism and copyright infringement. Librarians and students should be especially careful when embedding media and documents from other sources on to the LibGuides platform. For a more detailed look at copyright laws in the United States and the United Kingdom, see Chapter 6.

Best practices for using the LibGuides platform in pedagogy

Now that the features and potential uses of the LibGuides platform have been discussed at length, teaching librarians should consider the following best practices for using the LibGuides platform in pedagogy.

Librarians who are considering purchasing the platform for use at their institution need first to determine whether the cost of implementation will be prohibitive. They should create trial accounts to get a feel for the system and discover any issues that may arise in the implementation of the platform. Teaching librarians may also consider conducting a pilot study on an anticipated use of LibGuides. For example, a teaching librarian who wants to use a course-specific guide in her instruction could first solicit input from colleagues and/or students prior to using the guide in class. This would allow the librarian to fix any mistakes, such as misdirected links or non-functioning embedded videos, before directing her class to use the guide. For more detailed information on conducting a pilot study, see Chapter 5.

Other considerations that librarians should keep in mind prior to purchasing LibGuides include the time needed to train librarians on use of the platform and to create, maintain, and market the guides. Remember that the time used for these endeavors takes librarians away from their other duties and responsibilities.

Once the decision to purchase the LibGuides platform has been made, librarians should consider creating a 'best practices' guide for use at their institution. This would be aimed at librarians and other collaborators and should contain style guidelines (the fonts, colors, types of boxes, etc. that should be used in each guide created on the institution's LibGuides platform) and instructional information such as how to embed media and link to catalog records. It may also include direction as to what materials should be included in certain guides and what to leave out. For example, a best practices guide may state that every guide created should include contact information and/or a chat box so patrons can request additional research assistance as needed. The best practices guide can be used to ensure consistency among guides at a particular institution no matter who creates them. To see examples of such guides created by librarians, see the LibGuides best practices site.[27]

In addition to creating a best practices guide, librarians should schedule training sessions on the platform for all potential collaborators. Remember that some librarians will require more extensive training than others. Librarians should also schedule regular maintenance of the guides to confirm that the information included is still accurate and all links to outside sources are in working order.

To ensure that the intended audience is actually accessing and using the guides, teaching librarians should develop evaluation tools. Guides should then be evaluated on a regular basis. If librarians find their intended audience is not using the guides, they should consider making changes to the guides themselves or the ways in which they are marketed.

For example, if the guides need more marketing, librarians should consider providing additional instructional sessions utilizing the guides, or linking to them on the institution's social networking sites.

Organization is key when creating guides on the LibGuides platform. Teaching librarians need to keep guides clean and uncluttered. For example, librarians should ensure the homepage of each guide is organized and only contains essential information so it is easy for patrons to find what they are looking for. Since patrons are unlikely to use the guides if they find them difficult to navigate, librarians should make sure that the tabs in the guides are easy to use and understand. Tabs must also be consistent among guides across the platform; for example, all subject guides that include links to databases should have a tab with the same label. One guide should not refer to the databases as 'electronic resources' while another calls them 'databases'.

Patrons will not use the guides unless they are aware of their availability and find them useful. Librarians should enlist the assistance of faculty to help market the guides to students: highlight important features of the guides to faculty, and include information on how to link to or embed guides in their course sites. They should consider using LibGuides to create a course guide that serves as a homepage to house all course materials, including related library materials and resources, and information on how to access these. Librarians and faculty should consider making the guides interactive by allowing students to contribute links to helpful resources. However, students must be instructed on appropriate postings, plagiarism, and copyright infringement. Librarians must be mindful of copyright laws; teaching librarians must obtain copyright permission from students before using the information students contribute to the guide. Librarians must also be careful not to link to or embed outside sources that contain infringing material.

Librarians who want to create guides for informal instruction should focus on answering recurring patron questions. Subject and instructional guides can be placed in convenient places throughout the library, such as in the stacks near related material. These guides can be in print, or accessed on patrons' mobile devices by scanning QR codes. Librarians who create subject guides should include links to items in the library's catalog, information on and links to relevant databases and other electronic resources, and links to outside sources on the topic. They may also want to create and embed video tutorials on how to conduct research in the subject area and how to use specific databases. These guides can then be used to assist patrons via face-to-face or virtual reference.

Conclusion

As stated in Chapter 1, Web 2.0 tools should offer equal access, improve communication, provide an adequate level of class organization, and meet the needs of both traditional and non-traditional students. The Web 2.0 tools available in the LibGuides platform do all of these things. They allow teaching librarians to present research resources and instruction to their students and other patrons in an interactive, organized package.

The training and support features that the LibGuides platform offers its users are extensive. Even librarians with little technological know-how can quickly learn how to use all the features available on the platform.

Teaching librarians can create guides for a variety of pedagogical uses, from formal class instruction via course-specific guides to informal reference help via general library and subject guides. As long as the guides are easy to use and marketed well, patrons will use them.

In conclusion, teaching librarians should carefully consider the following prior to purchasing and implementing the LibGuides platform.

- Decide whether the cost of implementing LibGuides will be prohibitive to the library's budget.

- Consider creating a free trial account to get a feel for the system. This may alert a librarian to any issues that might arise in the implementation of the platform.

- Attempt to determine how much time will be needed to set up the system and train all collaborating librarians on use of the platform. Remember, not all librarians are tech savvy, and some will need more extensive instruction than others.

- Consider the time it takes not only to create but also to maintain and market each guide.

- Determine whether the intended audience will use the guides. It may be necessary to create an evaluation tool to confirm they are being used. Librarians may also need to provide more instruction sessions to make students aware of the availability of the guides and how to use them.

- Consider the time needed to make sure all materials posted on the LibGuides platform, including embedded videos, links to outside sources, and uploaded documents, do not violate any copyright laws or include plagiarized material.

Notes

1. LibGuides, 'Clients'; available at: *www.springshare.com/ libguides/clients.html* (accessed: 10 January 2013).
2. LibGuides, 'Features'; available at: *www.springshare.com/ libguides/features.html* (accessed: 10 January 2013).
3. Ibid.
4. LibGuides, 'Help'; available at: *http://help.springshare.com/ index.php?gid=179* (accessed: 10 January 2013).
5. LibGuides, 'Customize'; available at: *http://help.springshare. com/customizelg* (accessed: 10 January 2013).
6. LibGuides, 'Community'; available at: *http://libguides.com/ community.php?m=i&ref=libguides.com* (accessed: 10 January 2013).
7. LibGuides, 'Best of'; available at: *http://bestof.libguides.com/* (accessed: 12 January 2013).
8. LibGuides, 'Mobile site builder'; available at: *http://help. springshare.com/msb?hs=a* (accessed: 12 January 2013).
9. LibGuides, 'Training'; available at: *http://help.springshare. com/training* (accessed: 12 January 2013).
10. LibGuides, 'Features', note 2 above.
11. Ghaphery, J. and White, E. (2012) 'Library use of web-based research guides', *Information Technology and Libraries*, March: 21–31.
12. McMullin, R. and Hutton, J. (2010) 'Web subject guides: virtual connections across the university community', *Journal of Library Administration*, 50: 789–97.
13. Reeb, B. and Gibbons, S. (2004) 'Students, librarians, and subject guides: improving a poor rate of return', *Portal: Libraries & the Academy*, 4(1): 123–30, at p. 128.
14. McMullin and Hutton, note 12 above.
15. LibGuides, 'DePauw University COMM 233 guide'; available at: *http://libguides.depauw.edu/comm233-howley* (accessed: 12 January 2013).
16. Neves, K. and Dooley, S. (2011) 'Using LibGuides to offer library service to undergraduate medical students based on the case-oriented problem solving curriculum model', *Journal of the Medical Library Association*, 99(1): 94–7.

17. ALA, 'Information literacy standards'; available at: *www.ala. org/acrl/standards/informationliteracycompetency* (accessed: 13 January 2013).

18. Yelinek, K., Neyer, L., Bressler, D., Coffta, M., and Magolis, D. (2010) 'Using LibGuides for an information literacy tutorial', *College & Research Libraries News*, 71(7): 352–5.

19. McMullin and Hutton, note 12 above.

20. LibGuides, 'Pricing'; available at: *www.springshare.com/ libguides/benefits.html* (accessed: 10 January 2013).

21. Leibiger, C. (2011) 'LibGuides on steroids: expanding the user base of LibGuides to support library instruction and justify workload', PowerPoint slides; available at: *http:// digitalcommons.macalester.edu/libtech_conf/2011/sessions/23/* (accessed: 12 January 2013).

22. LibGuides, 'LibAnswers'; available at: *http://springshare. com/libanswers/* (accessed: 12 January 2013).

23. McMullin and Hutton, note 12 above.

24. Ibid.; Staley, S. (2007) 'Academic subject guides: a case study of use at San Jose State University', *College & Research Libraries*, March: 119–39.

25. Staley, ibid.

26. Ouellette, D. (2011) 'Subject guides in academic libraries: a user-centered study of uses and perceptions', *Canadian Journal of Information and Library Science*, 35(4): 436–51.

27. LibGuides, 'Best practices'; available at: *http://bestof.libguides. com/bestpractices* (accessed: 12 January 2013).

3

Cloud computing for teaching librarians

Abstract: This chapter defines and explains cloud computing, describing its recent popularity in pedagogy and its relevance in the future. It highlights specific types of cloud computing platforms that are available and the collaborative features of each. The chapter describes best practices for pedagogical use of cloud computing for teaching librarians, and examines its use at specific institutions. Additionally, it discusses important considerations, such as security, access, and reliability, of which teaching librarians need to be aware prior to implementing cloud computing in their instruction.

Key words: cloud computing, Dropbox, Google Calendar, Google Drive, Google Docs, Google Sites, SlideShare, Padlet, privacy, security.

Introduction

Cloud computing is being utilized more and more in pedagogy these days for several reasons: it facilitates student and instructor collaboration, it makes distance education easier to conduct, and it allows access to and editing of course documents from practically any location. In addition to fostering collaboration and easy access, cloud computing allows for scalability by offering teaching librarians nearly unlimited storage space for relatively minimal cost.

Many people have been using cloud-based web services for years without realizing they were doing so. For example, anyone who uses web-based email services such as Gmail and Yahoo! accesses his email, contacts, and calendars via cloud computing. Social networking sites such as Facebook, blogging sites like Twitter, and video-sharing sites such as YouTube are all also examples of cloud-based computing. A number of the Web 2.0 pedagogical tools discussed throughout this book use cloud computing components, including the LibGuides platform and Moodle, as do many of the mobile apps discussed in Chapter 4.

While cloud computing is a great tool to facilitate learning and foster collaboration, librarians need to be aware of the downsides to using it in their instruction. Security, reliability, and access issues as well as user training and copyright implications are top concerns for teaching librarians who wish to implement cloud-based computing.

Cloud computing defined and explained

The National Institute of Standards and Technology, a division of the US Department of Commerce, defines cloud computing as:

> A model for enabling ubiquitous, convenient, on-demand network access to a shared pool of configurable computing resources (e.g., networks, servers, storage, applications, and services) that can be rapidly provisioned and released with minimal management effort or service provider interaction.[1]

Cloud providers offer their customers three service models: software as a service (SaaS), platform as a service (PaaS), and infrastructure as a service (IaaS).[2] The SaaS model allows users to interact solely with the cloud provider's application; the PaaS model allows users to develop applications with the cloud provider's tools; and the IaaS model allows users to control virtual servers and choose the amount of storage they need. This means customers of a specific cloud service provider can use the cloud's platform to access software and applications created by the cloud provider, the customer, or a third party; and the cloud service provides the storage and processing needs of those applications. Customers do not have to worry about purchasing specific hardware or having enough storage space on their networks or computers to install, run, and update software; the cloud service provider handles all of these tasks itself.

Mell and Grance[3] describe four distinct types of cloud deployment models: private, community, public, and hybrid. Private clouds are created for and used by a single entity. Community clouds are created for and used by multiple related entities. Public clouds are created for and used by the general public. Hybrid clouds are any combination of the first three deployment models. Most of the cloud systems discussed in this chapter use the public cloud deployment model.

Many cloud service providers permit multiple users to access and edit documents stored in the cloud by allowing the documents to be shared across the platform. Any changes made to the shared document are accessible to all users sharing the document. Cloud computing also permits easy backup of files. Generally speaking, a user simply saves the document to the cloud platform and a backup is created; the user does not need to back up the file on a local storage device. Users of cloud systems can access their saved files from virtually anywhere they have access to a web browser. Additionally, some cloud service providers offer offline access to files and data stored on their platforms. A more detailed look into specific cloud service providers and their system features is given later in this chapter.

Relevance of cloud computing

A 2010 Pew Internet survey of nearly 900 technology experts (with ties to companies like Google, Microsoft, IBM, Thomson Reuters, and the *New York Times*, as well as many US federal agencies and universities) found that by the next decade most people will be using cloud-based applications and services in lieu of software and hardware stored on local networks and personal computers.[4] The experts indicated that the surge in use of handheld devices such as mobile phones and tablets will increase the production and use of web-based applications. In fact, several agreed that many people already do most of their computing in the cloud. As people get used to being able to access their documents and applications from practically anywhere they have an internet connection, no matter what device they are using, they will expect this access to continue and expand.

Cloud computing is so prevalent today that tech companies are creating devices which work almost entirely in the cloud. For example, the Google Chromebook[5] allows users to access thousands of web-based applications in lieu of locally stored software. People simply choose the applications they want to use, and have near-instant access to those tools. Additionally, all necessary updates occur automatically. Because there is no software to install and most information and applications are stored in the cloud (via Google Drive and other cloud services), these devices boot up extremely fast and have a relatively long battery life. The lack of on-site storage means the devices are more affordable than laptop or desktop computers. The Google Chromebook starts at about US$249 (£164). Due to the availability and affordability of such cloud-based devices, more and more students will be using them and the web-based applications that run on them.

Teaching librarians must not only be aware of the prevalence of cloud computing in their students' and patrons' daily lives but also be able to utilize cloud-based systems in their instruction. The following sections discuss uses and examples of specific cloud-based services available to teaching librarians.

Uses for teaching librarians and examples of specific cloud services available

Cloud computing lends itself to pedagogy because it allows affordable, on-demand access to files and data. As Stein et al.[6] state in their case study, cloud computing gives more choices in pedagogical software and vast savings on software licensing, both of which allow greater freedom in instruction. Instead of using an expensive course management software program, teaching librarians can implement cloud services to house and share with students all course documents, assignments, outside readings, and presentations. Librarians can also foster interactive learning by having students collaborate on coursework by editing and updating files stored in the cloud. Group projects become easier to manage, since group members no longer need to be in the same physical location to collaborate on an assignment. This fosters asynchronous learning and eliminates geographical and time barriers.

Stein et al.[7] describe an educational cloud service created by North Carolina State University called the Virtual Computing Lab. Their case study focuses on the use of this cloud service in rural high school mathematics classes. The students at these North Carolina schools have access to school-provided laptops and broadband internet. Two specific programs were used in geometry and algebra classes: The Geometer's Sketchpad 5 and Fathom 2 (both available from Key Curriculum Press[8]). These programs allowed students to collaborate on their math assignments and receive instant feedback from their teachers. Instruction and class work became more collaborative and interactive as a result of using the Virtual Computing Lab. Teachers did not have to worry about maintaining and updating the programs used in their classes, since the providers of the Virtual Computing Lab updated and maintained the programs themselves.

Teaching librarians can utilize similar educational-centered cloud services to meet the needs of their students and provide a more interactive and collaborative learning environment. By storing, maintaining, and updating software on a cloud service, instructors can offer more program and course material options without forcing their students to incur additional expenses.

There are many cloud service providers available to teaching librarians. Below are descriptions some of the most-used service providers, and information about the features they offer and how teaching librarians can best use those features and services.

Dropbox

A basic Dropbox.com (*https://www.dropbox.com/*) account give users 2GB of storage for free, with up to 18GB total free storage with referrals. Users can update to Pro or Team accounts that offer a significant amount of extra storage for an annual fee ranging from around US$795 (£521) for five users to about $31,420 (£20,500) for 250 users.[9] Dropbox allows its users to sync their files across all their devices (laptops, desktops, mobile phones, and tablets). Files can be shared with both non-users and users alike. All users accessing shared files will automatically be able to access the most up-to-date version of the files. Dropbox offers a range of security features, from deletion recovery to extensive encryption.[10] It also has a help center,[11] which less tech-savvy teaching librarians and students can access to learn more about using the service.

Since a basic Dropbox account is free, librarians can have their students sign up for accounts to use in class. Teaching librarians can create a shared course folder to store all course-related documents, photos, and videos that they want their students to manipulate. Students can also create their own shared folders and files for group projects, where only members of a specific group have access to the documents.

If a teaching librarian does not want to make students sign up for Dropbox accounts, she can create a link to specific files and folders in Dropbox and share that link via the course website, email, Facebook, or Twitter.[12] This allows non-Dropbox users to access course materials without having to create accounts.

Teaching librarians must be careful not to post copyrighted material to their Dropbox folders without proper permission from the copyright owner. They should also instruct their students on the basics of copyright laws and plagiarism, and monitor student postings to ensure that there are no cases of copyright infringement or plagiarism in the students' work.

Google Docs, Drive, Sites, and more

Google offers a host of cloud-based services, from Google Drive to Google Sites, all of which are free to implement at their basic levels. Many librarians are probably already familiar with Google Docs, which was once a stand-alone service. It is now part of Google Drive (*https://drive.google.com/*), Google's answer to Dropbox.com. Similar to Dropbox, Google Drive allows users to access and store documents and data remotely. Users get 5GB of storage for free and can pay monthly for extra storage, ranging from 25GB for about US$2.49 (£1.60) up to 16TB for about $799 (£524).[13]

Teaching librarians can share documents and files with their students and choose whether students are able to view the documents, edit them, or comment on them; each document can have its own settings based on the teacher's needs. This allows the teaching librarian to share all course documents with the students, but prevents students from changing documents like the syllabus while simultaneously allowing them to collaborate on other files, such as group assignments. Google Drive also allows users to view documents from various programs directly in their browsers, which means students do not need to have those programs installed on their computers.[14] Google Drive encourages teaching librarians and students to collaborate on documents, spreadsheets, and presentations. It tracks all edits and changes, so everyone can see who made what changes, and allows students to engage with each other by creating comments on the document. This fosters peer evaluation and ensures that students have a more interactive educational experience.

Google Sites (*https://sites.google.com/*) is another cloud-based service that allows users to create websites and wikis. Teaching librarians can use it to create a course site to house all course information. Google Sites can be used in collaboration with other Google products. For example, teaching librarians can upload collaborative Google Docs to their Google Sites course site. They can also embed an interactive course calendar in their sites using Google Calendar (see the following paragraph for more information). Teachers can include other Web 2.0 tools, like videos and podcasts, by linking to or embedding the material in their sites. They can create RSS feeds for their course sites, to which students can subscribe to receive daily updates on changes to the sites. Google Sites is relatively easy to use and allows teaching librarians to create their own sites or choose from various ready-made templates.[15] In addition to a course site, librarians can create a wiki on Google Sites, where students contribute to the content as a course assignment. More detailed information about creating and using wikis in pedagogy can be found in Chapter 1.

In addition to the above cloud-based Google services, teaching librarians can use Google Calendar (*https://www. google.com/calendar/*) to create and share a course calendar with students. Librarians can set up reminders for assignments, tests, and appointments. Since the calendar is web-based and allows syncing with mobile devices, students can access it at any time from anywhere they have an internet connection, and will always access the most up-to-date information.[16] Google Calendar also allows offline access, so students can view the calendar even when they do not have internet access.

As with Dropbox, teaching librarians must be careful not to post copyrighted material to their Google Docs, Drive, Sites, or other applications without proper permission from the copyright owner. They should also instruct their students on the basics of copyright laws and plagiarism, and monitor student postings to ensure there are no cases of copyright infringement or plagiarism in the students' work.

SlideShare

Librarians can use the cloud-based program SlideShare (*www.slideshare.net/*) to make their presentations accessible to students outside of the classroom. SlideShare allows teachers to share documents, PDFs, videos, and webinars with their students. Presentations and webinars created with SlideShare can be linked to social networking sites such as Facebook and Twitter, and accessed on mobile devices.[17] SlideShare also allows librarians to conduct virtual meetings with students by way of Zipcast, which includes slides, audio, video, and chat.[18] The free version of SlideShare allows public Zipcast meetings, while an upgraded version, SlideShare Pro, allows private, password-protected Zipcast meetings. Users can upgrade to SlideShare Pro for about US$19 (£12.50) per month.[19] SlideShare gives educational discounts for annual subscriptions.

Again, teaching librarians should be aware of copyright laws and potential infringement on behalf of their students and themselves when uploading documents, videos, and audio files to SlideShare presentations.

Padlet

Padlet (*http://padlet.com*), formerly called Wallwisher, allows teaching librarians to create incredibly collaborative and interactive learning environments for their students for free. Teachers can post content to a blank space called a wall, then share their walls with students via RSS feeds, social networking sites, email links, or embedding them into a course website. Students can participate in discussions, question-and-answer threads, brainstorming sessions, and other group activities. The moderation function allows teachers to ensure that student posts adhere to all course policies and do not include plagiarism or copyright infringement.

In addition to creating content on their walls, librarians can embed Web 2.0 content from outside sources to share with their students. Videos, podcasts, and blogging platforms such as WordPress or Moodle can be embedded into course walls. Walls created on Padlet are extremely user friendly, so even the least tech-savvy teaching librarians and students can use the site with little assistance or training. Padlet is available on all modern web browsers, and most features are available on mobile devices as well. That means students and teaching librarians can access and post content to course walls from practically anywhere they have an internet connection. All content posted to a wall is stored remotely, so teaching librarians do not need to worry about their walls becoming full; there is always more room to post additional content.[20]

Which option to choose

In conclusion, teaching librarians can consider using the following cloud-based services for these specific activities.

- Dropbox can be used to house course materials and allow student collaboration on documents.

- Google Sites can be used in conjunction with Google Drive, Google Docs, and Google Calendar to create and host a course website where students can collaborate on documents and spreadsheets, access an interactive course calendar, and view Web 2.0 tools such as videos, links, and podcasts.

- SlideShare can be used to provide access to presentations, webinars, and other documents outside of class; SlideShare can also be used to host virtual meetings or appointments with students using the Zipcast feature.

- Padlet can be used in numerous ways, from hosting discussion threads and brainstorming sessions to embedding videos and blog posts.

Considerations: access, security and privacy, reliability, and training

Prior to implementing any of these cloud computing services in their instruction, teaching librarians should carefully consider the following issues. Because most service providers require an active internet connection to access information stored on the cloud platform, librarians need to ensure students have access to the internet outside of the classroom or library. While most collaboration and interaction with the cloud services may occur in class, these otherwise engaging and interactive tools are useless in situations like distance education if students cannot access them and collaborate outside class. Teaching librarians should also ensure that students can access the cloud-based tools at no additional cost.

One of the recurring themes in the respondents' remarks in the 2010 Pew Internet survey of technology experts was that of security and privacy issues in cloud computing.[21] Because information in cloud platforms is stored remotely, the creators of the information cannot ensure it is secure and remains private. Instead, they must rely on third parties to protect their information. Teaching librarians must keep this in mind and consider whether they want to entrust their course materials and student assignments to third-party providers. Content can be lost in a variety of ways, from elaborate hacking operations to basic platform malfunction. Most cloud services provide extensive safeguards to ensure user information is kept secure and private. For example, Dropbox employs Secure Sockets Layer (SSL) and AES-256 bit encryption to protect user files, and Amazon's Simple Storage Service (S3) to back up and store user data and files.[22] However, even with these safeguards in place, due to security and privacy concerns librarians may need to get approval from their institutions prior to utilizing cloud computing in instruction. Some institutions may have policies in place discouraging the use of cloud computing due to student privacy concerns.

If a teaching librarian implements a cloud-based service as a main component of a course, that service must be reliable. Since the cloud services are maintained and updated by third-party providers, users have no control over when features are updated or platform maintenance is performed. Any updates or maintenance may cause certain features or even the entire service to be unavailable to users for an extended period of time. This could negatively impact students' use and perception of the cloud-based service, which could in turn result in poor participation.

A final point of consideration for teaching librarians wishing to utilize cloud computing is that of training users on the various systems. While most of the cloud systems discussed in this chapter are fairly user friendly and easy, some librarians and even some students (especially non-traditional students) may need training on proper use of all interactive and collaborative features available to them. Teaching librarians need to consider whether the benefits of using a particular cloud service outweigh the time it takes to set up, maintain, and train themselves and their students on the use of the service.

In conclusion, prior to implementing any of these cloud computing services, teaching librarians should carefully consider the following issues.

- Ensure students have access to the internet and cloud-based services outside class, and that access to the tools does not incur additional cost for students.

- Be aware that the materials hosted on cloud-based platforms are at risk for security and privacy breaches, and users must rely on third parties to ensure the security of their documents.

- Keep in mind that not all cloud-based services provide the same level of reliability, and things such as maintenance and updates are out of your control.

- Consider the amount of training needed by all users prior to implementing a particular cloud-based service.

Best practices for using cloud computing in pedagogy

Librarians who want to implement cloud computing in their teaching should note some best practices. First, they should consider conducting a pilot study on an anticipated use of a cloud-based service. For example, a librarian who wants to create a course site using Google Sites could solicit input from colleagues regarding the site. This would allow the teacher to ensure all content on the site functions properly, including embedded documents, calendars, and videos, prior to allowing students to view and interact with the site in and out of class. Teaching librarians should use the pilot study to ensure that not only content works properly, but also the cloud service is user friendly. The pilot can help teachers identify any areas that may require additional training for users, especially non-traditional students. For more detailed information on conducting a pilot study, see Chapter 5.

Teaching librarians should be sure to keep all course materials posted on cloud-based services organized and easy to use. In addition, they should set up all collaborative cloud files for the course and post clearly stated policies on proper student use and behavior when contributing content to interactive cloud-based course materials. Specifically, librarians should inform students about what is and is not proper to post to course materials, remind them about plagiarism, and instruct them on the basics of copyright infringement. Teaching librarians should monitor all student activity on the cloud-based services. Many of the services discussed in this chapter allow users to track who adds what content to a particular document. This way librarians can ensure all students are participating equally and following all course policies. Teachers should deduct class points for repeat violations of any of the above policies.

Students are not the only users who must be mindful of copyright laws; teaching librarians must obtain permission from students for future use of the information and materials they contribute to collaborative cloud-based course assignments. Librarians must also be careful not to link to or embed outside sources that contain infringing material. For a more detailed look at copyright laws in the United States and the United Kingdom, see Chapter 6.

Teaching librarians should implement cloud-based services to encourage students to collaborate and interact with their peers by sharing rich information, such as videos, audio files, and links to outside sources. They should also encourage students not just to receive this information passively, but to be critical of it and constructively evaluate their peers' contributions to group assignments.

In conclusion, teaching librarians should consider the following best practices prior to utilizing cloud-based services in their instruction.

- Conduct a pilot study for the intended use of a cloud-based service to ensure all features function properly and identify areas that require additional user training.

- Ensure information included in a course-specific cloud service is organized and easy to access.

- Post policies on proper student use and behavior when contributing content to interactive cloud-based course materials, including information about plagiarism and the basics of copyright infringement.

- Monitor student activity by tracking edits, comments, and additions to collaborative documents.

- Be mindful of the copyright implications of the librarian's own contributions to cloud platforms.

- Encourage collaboration and critical thinking by allowing students to evaluate their peers' contributions to cloud-based course materials.

Conclusion

Cloud computing offers teaching librarians many ways to improve their instruction: it facilitates student and instructor collaboration, it makes distance education easier to conduct, and it allows access to and editing of course documents from practically any location. In addition to fostering collaboration and ease of access, cloud computing allows for scalability by offering teaching librarians nearly unlimited storage space for relatively minimal cost.

Cloud computing allows teachers to utilize many Web 2.0 tools, such as collaborative documents, embedded videos, and audio files, in classes. Many cloud-based services are free to use and upgrades are often fairly inexpensive. Because cloud computing services such as web-based email, social networking sites, and video-sharing sites are already prevalent today, many students and librarians will need little instruction on how to use these in their courses.

Of course, all the benefits of cloud computing come with inherent risks, including security and privacy breaches, ease and cost of access for students, reliability across platforms, and copyright implications. Teaching librarians must carefully calculate the risks and benefits of a cloud-based system prior to implementing it in their instruction.

Notes

1. Mell, O. and Grance, T. (2011) 'The NIST definition of cloud computing', Special Publication 800-145, September, National Institute of Standards and Technology, US Department of Commerce; available at: *http://csrc.nist.gov/publications/ nistpubs/800-145/SP800-145.pdf* (accessed: 15 December 2012).
2. Bala, P. (2010) 'Intensification of educational cloud computing and crisis of data security in public clouds', *International Journal on Computer Science and Engineering*, 2(3): 741–5.
3. Mell and Grance, note 1 above.
4. Anderson, J. and Rainie, L. (2010) 'The future of cloud computing', Pew Internet, June; available at: *http://pewinternet. org/Reports/2010/The-future-of-cloud-computing.aspx* (accessed: 15 December 2012).
5. Google Chromebook, 'Features'; available at: *www.google. com/intl/en/chrome/devices/features-learnmore.html* (accessed: 5 February 2013).
6. Stein, S., Ware, J., Laboy, J., and Schaffer, H. (2013) 'Improving K-12 pedagogy via a cloud designed for education', *International Journal of Information Management*, 33: 235–41.
7. Ibid.

8. Key Curriculum, 'Products'; available at: *www.keycurriculum.com/products* (accessed: 5 February 2013).

9. Dropbox, 'Pricing'; available at: *https://www.dropbox.com/pricing* (accessed: 6 February 2013).

10. Dropbox, 'Security'; available at: *https://www.dropbox.com/dmca#security* (accessed: 6 February 2013).

11. Dropbox, 'Help'; available at: *https://www.dropbox.com/help* (accessed: 6 February 2013).

12. Dropbox, 'Sharing files'; available at: *https://www.dropbox.com/help/20/en* (accessed: 6 February 2013).

13. Google Drive, 'Pricing'; available at: *https://support.google.com/drive/bin/answer.py?hl=en&answer=2375123&p=mktg_pricing* (accessed: 6 February 2013).

14. Google Drive, 'Features'; available at: *https://www.google.com/intl/en_US/drive/start/features.html* (accessed: 7 February 2013).

15. Google Sites, 'Overview'; available at: *www.google.com/sites/help/intl/en/overview.html* (accessed: 7 February 2013).

16. Google Calendar, 'About'; available at: *http://support.google.com/calendar/bin/answer.py?hl=en&answer=2465776* (accessed: 7 February 2013).

17. SlideShare, 'About'; available at: *www.slideshare.net/about* (accessed: 7 February 2013).

18. SlideShare, 'Introducing Zipcast'; available at: *www.slideshare.net/rashmi/introducing-zipcast* (accessed: 7 February 2013).

19. SlideShare, 'Premium plans'; available at: *www.slideshare.net/business/premium/plans?cmp_src=footer* (accessed: 7 February 2013).

20. Padlet, 'What do I do when my wall is full?'; available at: *http://jn.padlet.com/knowledgebase/articles/167882-what-do-i-do-when-my-wall-is-full-* (accessed: 7 February 2013).

21. Anderson and Rainie, note 4 above.

22. Dropbox, 'How secure is Dropbox?'; available at: *https://www.dropbox.com/help/27/en* (accessed: 7 February 2013).

4

Mobile apps for teaching librarians

Abstract: This chapter discusses the use of mobile apps, highlighting specific apps that are available to teaching librarians and describing the features as well as the benefits and potential drawbacks of using each app in pedagogy and other areas. The chapter notes important considerations, such as security, reliability, availability, and cost, of which teaching librarians need to be aware prior to using mobile apps in their instruction. Additionally, it describes best practices for the pedagogical use of mobile apps.

Key words: mobile apps, applications, app builders, library apps, reference apps, mobile learning, mobile devices.

Introduction

Simply put, mobile applications are software programs that run on devices such as mobile phones or tablets. According to a recent comScore report, in 2012 smartphones made up over 50 percent of the mobile phone market for the first time in history.[1] People rely on their smartphones and the mobile applications, or apps, on them every day to organize their lives and make tasks easier to complete. These apps are so prevalent in today's society that the Apple App Store alone has recorded over 40 billion total mobile app downloads.[2]

There are many uses for mobile apps in the realm of education and pedagogy. For example, they can be used to organize documents and information for class, to take attendance, and to hold virtual conferences or appointments with students. Most cloud service providers also have mobile applications that their clients can use to access documents stored in the cloud from their mobile devices.

Mobile apps lend themselves to distance education due to their mobility; students can interact and collaborate with each other and their instructors despite not being in the same physical location. They foster interactivity, since many allow students to manipulate images displayed on the screen of mobile devices. Apps also foster collaboration, because multiple users can edit documents and track each change made to a particular document. This allows students to evaluate each other in an informal way. Many apps even allow multiple users to communicate with each other via chat or video capabilities.

While mobile apps have the ability to make organizing for class and presenting information to students easier and more interactive, teaching librarians should consider things like cost, privacy, security, reliability, and availability prior to utilizing these apps in their instruction.

Uses for teaching librarians

Articles, presentations, and blog posts about pedagogical uses for mobile apps and devices are abundant.[3] Most literature on this topic lists specific apps or mobile devices and how to use them to improve class interactivity, collaboration, and/or organization. For example, in her blog 'Technology Teacher' Dr Barbara Schroeder of Boise State University lists ten ways to use iPads in the classroom:

(1) Load iPads with eBooks and then select and assign reading groups for certain books. Simply hand the iPad to a group of students and have them read a book together. (2) Select movies to view and again, hand them to groups of students. Then, have them use the iPad to write to a class blog or online course site, responding to discussion prompts. (3) Use the iPad just like any Internet-connected computer, having students use Google Docs (install the Google Mobile apps) for collaborative writing and multimedia creation activities. (4) Have students search for podcasts in iTunes on a topic of study and listen to them on the iPad. (5) Subscribe to various periodicals and newspapers on the iPad and include a daily reading and discussion period. (6) Watch any number of quality online shows, searching by the topic of study, bookmarking and maintaining a list and critique of sources. (7) Research the various iPad apps and have students list and critique them, creating an online resource guide for the iPad and school activities using Google Sites. (8) Try out various Twitter apps for the iPad, such as TweetFlow and set up a class Twitter account to keep track of activities throughout the school year. (9) Purchase the Keynote app and teach your students how to prepare professional presentations, using multimedia learning principles. (10) Learn along with your students and take a class on iPhone and mobile development, working on an iPad app for your school.[4]

Most of the educational uses of the iPad that Dr Schroeder suggests can also be achieved on laptop or desktop computers. The iPad and the mobile apps loaded on it simply make these tasks more portable and easier to use in a group setting.

In their article on creating an iPad lending program at the University of Cincinnati, Johnston and Stoll suggest more effective pedagogical uses of iPads and mobile apps.[5] For example, teaching librarians should take their iPad or other mobile device with them as they move around the classroom, explaining problems and showing students answers and examples on the iPad or device. Johnston and Stoll believe that pedagogy, as opposed to technology, is still the most important element in classroom instruction, but also that effective use of mobile devices and applications can make learning more interactive and foster student collaboration.

In her article discussing mobile learning, Franklin states that mobile devices and applications do not change how people learn; rather, they allow for active learning by students through interaction and reflection.[6] For students to reach higher levels of learning, Franklin states that mobile learning should provide students with individualized experiences, freedom to make mistakes, continuous access to course information, and the ability to communicate, collaborate, and share with classmates and instructors.

The following sections provide examples of specific types of mobile applications that teaching librarians can utilize both in their instruction and for organization. Apps are separated into categories based on specific uses. Information about the features and cost, as well as any major benefits of use, is included. Many of these apps foster higher levels of learning by encouraging collaboration, interactivity, and evaluation. This list is by no means exhaustive; rather it serves to show examples of mobile apps that may be useful for teaching librarians in a variety of ways. Price and availability of each application vary by region, but many similar apps at a variety of price ranges can be found on app store websites. When choosing mobile apps, teaching librarians should consider cost and read reviews of the apps to ensure that each fits the instructor's specific needs. Best practices for using mobile apps in pedagogy and more detailed points for consideration are included in later sections of this chapter.

Apps geared toward libraries in general

This section features two general apps geared to libraries and their patrons. While they may not be the most useful apps for teaching librarians to utilize in their instruction, they offer beneficial features to libraries and patrons.

Boopsie

Unlike the rest of the apps presented in this chapter, Boopsie (*www.boopsie.com*) creates a customized app for a specific library – it is not an app itself. It is included here because it offers many very useful features for patrons, teaching librarians, and students alike.

According to its website, over 2,500 libraries worldwide utilize Boopsie. Boopsie offers many services, one of which is creating mobile apps for individual libraries.[7] While many libraries have mobile versions of their websites, mobile apps generally provide more interactivity and usability. There are two packages from which to choose: standard and optimum. Pricing depends on the size of the library, but purchasing the library's app itself is generally free for users. The standard package allows patrons to search the catalog, access their accounts (to view checkouts, place holds on items, etc.), contact a reference librarian (via text, email, or phone), interact with the library's social networking sites, and even check out materials using their mobile devices.[8] The optimum package includes all the standard features plus allowing patrons to view eBooks, access reviews, and find out whether books at a bookstore are available at the library.[9]

While its main benefits are geared toward library patrons, teaching librarians can use this app to highlight resources available in the library. Because it allows patrons to contact a reference librarian at the touch of a button, students have easy access to their instructors when working on research assignments. Teachers can also have their students access and read eBooks directly from the Boopsie app. The app is useful for teaching librarians who want to see whether particular materials they need for class are available at the institution's library.

LibAnywhere

LibAnywhere (*www.libanywhere.com*) is another app that allows patrons to access library information such as catalogs, hours, branches, and events, and to contact reference librarians. It is available for mobile devices that run on the Apple iOS and devices that run on the Android platform. There is also a version compatible with any device that can access the internet.[10] The app itself is available for download free of charge.

Similar to custom apps from Boopsie, teaching librarians can have their students use the LibAnywhere app to find resources in the library quickly and contact reference librarians when working on research assignments.

Apps for taking and organizing notes

As the heading indicates, the apps listed in this section are useful for taking and organizing notes, but they also allow users to manipulate these notes and one of the apps allows users to collect and organize other types of information as well. They foster collaboration, since multiple users can access and manipulate shared notes.

Catch

Catch (*https://catch.com*) offers free and paid apps for Apple iOS and Android mobile devices. The apps allow users to create notes (via text, voice, or video) and save them to 'spaces'. The basic free plan offers users three spaces, which can be private or shared with other users, and 70MB of content per month.[11] The Pro plan offers users 50 spaces (again, these can be private or shared with other users) and 1GB of content per month; it costs about US$4.99 (£3) per month or $44.99 (£29) per year. The Premier plan, offered at about $15.99 (£10.50) monthly or $144.99 (£95) yearly, gives users 200 spaces (private or shared) and 5GB of content per month. In all plans, users can organize their notes by assigning them different tags. Users can also back up all their notes by syncing them to Catch's cloud storage website, catch.com, and protect notes by creating pass codes.[12] Users can safely collaborate on shared spaces with other Catch users, and any revisions to shared spaces are updated across all users' devices.

Teaching librarians can use Catch to organize group projects and get their students to collaborate on assignments. Students can create checklists and reminders for due dates. Since all revisions are marked on Catch, students can use the app to evaluate their peers' contributions to group work. The free plan is ideal to use, as it carries no additional cost to teaching librarians or students. As the app works on both Apple iOS and Android mobile devices, most students would be able to use it. Students who do not own mobiles can still access group spaces by logging on to catch.com to get the synced notes.

EverNote

EverNote (*http://evernote.com*) is similar to Catch in that it allows users to save notes and sync them across multiple mobile devices and personal computers. However, EverNote allows users to save more than just notes; they can also save full webpages or portions of pages by clipping them. Users can take photos with their mobile devices' built-in cameras or record audio with their mobiles' microphones and save those files in their EverNote app. EverNote allows users to collaborate with others by sharing their notes. The app is available free for both Android and Apple iOS devices. Users can upgrade to a premium account for about US$5 (£3) per month or $45 (£29) per year. The premium version allows users to upload more documents each month, view past versions of notes, and collaborate more effectively by allowing multiple users to edit notes.[13]

Teaching librarians can use the EverNote app to organize documents and videos that may be useful in class. They can also collaborate with students on notes or have students collaborate with each other. Like Catch, EverNote has a companion website, so students can access their notes either from their mobile devices using the app or from their personal desktop or laptop computers.

Apps for organizing ideas and resources

The apps featured in this category allow students and teaching librarians to organize ideas and information like citations. The first and last apps listed are great collaborative tools, while the second is very useful for keeping track of and organizing research sources.

Inspiration Maps

Inspiration Maps (*https://itunes.apple.com/us/app/inspiration-maps/id510173686?mt=8*) is available for Apple iOS mobile devices and is designed specifically as an educational tool for the iPad. It is a great application for creating mind maps and other diagrams. The application costs roughly US$9.99 (£6.60), so it may be too expensive for each student to buy individually. However, discounts are available through Apple's volume purchase plan for educational endeavors.[14] There is also a 'lite' version that users can try for free prior to purchasing the full app. Users can create an unlimited number of maps using a variety of templates. Some templates are available in Spanish as well as UK English. Users can attach documents and photos to their maps and share maps with others using iTunes or Dropbox.

This is an especially useful tool for teaching librarians who want students to engage in collaborating and brainstorming activities. Making maps on the app is very simple and takes little instruction. It may be cost prohibitive to require all students to purchase the app, and many may not have access to iPads outside class. The instructor may be able to acquire a handful of iPads and load the app on to them for student use in class. Even if just one iPad is available it could be circulated to different groups within the class to use at assigned times.

EasyBib

EasyBib (*www.easybib.com*), a free mobile app available for Apple iOS and Android mobile devices, allows users to create bibliographies using MLA (Modern Language Association), APA (American Psychological Association), and Chicago style citation formats. Users can simply scan a book's barcode with their mobile device's built-in camera to add the book's citation information to their works-cited list.

If no barcode is accessible, users can manually input citation information. EasyBib will automatically put the citation in the correct MLA, APA, or Chicago style format; the user simply chooses which format he needs. Users can then email the citations to themselves to include in their assignments.

This is an especially useful mobile application for both teaching librarians and their students. Teachers can use the app for their own scholarship and also to check their students' works-cited lists. They can recommend this app to classes to ensure students turn in properly cited assignments. The company that created the app has a companion website with more extensive citation tools and provides resources for educators and librarians.[15]

Trello

Trello (*https://trello.com*) is a great collaboration tool. It allows users to create cards with different tasks on them and organize the cards into various lists on their boards. The cards can include due dates and notes, and users can attach documents, photos, and videos to them. Users can add collaborators who can add notes to cards and work together in real time. Tasks can be assigned to different collaborators and users can set up email notifications and reminders.[16] Trello works across platforms and is formatted for all screen sizes. The website and mobile app are both free to use and the mobile app is available for both Apple iOS and Android devices.

Teaching librarians can use Trello to create a course board for all course projects and assign students to different groups. Students can work together to create checklists and due dates, and assign tasks to different group members. Because all changes to a card or board are marked, students can evaluate their group mates' contributions to assignments. This app fosters collaboration and teaches students to work together and evaluate each other's contributions.

Cloud computing apps

The following two mobile apps are the companion applications to the cloud computing platforms discussed in Chapter 3. They are especially useful for teaching librarians who already store documents and course materials to either of the corresponding cloud platforms.

Dropbox and Google Drive

The full versions of these two platforms are discussed in detail in Chapter 3; both have corresponding mobile apps that allow users to access their documents stored in the cloud from anywhere using mobile devices. Both the Dropbox (*https://www.dropbox.com*) and Google Drive (*https://www.google.com/intl/en_US/drive/start/index.html*) mobile apps are free for users to download and available for Apple iOS and Android mobile devices.

Both these mobile apps allow teaching librarians to create a shared course folder to store all course-related documents, photos, and videos that they want their students to manipulate. Students can also create their own shared folders and files for group projects, where only members of a specific group have access to the documents. Teaching librarians and students can then access these documents anywhere directly from the mobile applications.

Apps for reading and researching

The apps listed below offer many beneficial features for teaching librarians and their students, ranging from accessing scholarly articles to reading eBooks and saving helpful webpages for later use. While some of the apps are designed for individual users, a couple offer opportunities for student collaboration.

AccessMyLibrary

AccessMyLibrary (*www.gale.cengage.com/apps/aml/ CollegeLibrary/*) is a free mobile app, available to both Android and Apple iOS users, that works in conjunction with a college or university library's Gale databases. Students and faculty log in with their university email addresses to access the online resources available to them from Gale. This allows students to find full-text articles from electronic journals and other scholarly publications and read them on their mobile devices. Teaching librarians whose libraries provide access to Gale databases can have their students use this app as another way to view those databases at any time from anywhere they have an internet connection.

ArticleSearch

ArticleSearch (*https://itunes.apple.com/us/app/articlesearch/ id401914624?mt=8*) is a free mobile app designed for Apple iOS devices. It allows users to search for scholarly articles and other academic publications. Users can perform basic or advanced searches, read abstracts, and even get the full text of articles. They have the option of saving articles or sharing them with others via email or text message.[17] Users can pay a fee to access premium search engines to get better results: they can pick up to three search engines for about US$1.99 (£1.31), up to seven for around $2.99 (£2), or unlimited for roughly $4.99 (£3).

Teaching librarians can use this app in conjunction with research projects given to their students. While it may not offer the extensive resources of an academic library's holdings, it is another tool at students' disposal.

Kindle

Kindle (*www.amazon.com/gp/feature.html?ie=UTF8&docI d=1000493771*) reading apps are compatible with Amazon's Kindle eBook reading devices. The app (free for both Apple iOS and Android mobile devices, as well as on a cloud platform) allows users to access and read any books they have purchased or borrowed from Amazon's Kindle store. Users can also check out eBooks from participating libraries, and access these from their Kindle app. Most books in the Kindle store cost around US$9.99 (£6.60), but there are also many books that are available free of charge.

Since this mobile app is free for users, runs on all devices, and can be accessed on any computer with an internet connection, it is a good tool for teaching librarians. Instructors can direct their students to download specific books to read for class. Many classic titles that are no longer covered by copyright laws are free to download. Students can also check out eBooks from libraries to read.

Instapaper and Pocket

Instapaper (*www.instapaper.com*) and Pocket (*http:// getpocket.com*) are two mobile apps that allow users to save webpages to read later. The Instapaper app is pretty basic: users simply click the 'Read Later' bookmark when browsing on the web to save that page. When they want to go back to view the webpage the link is available in their Instapaper app. Instapaper costs about US$3.99 (£2.60) and is designed to run on Apple iPhones and iPads. Pocket is a free mobile app that is available for both Apple iOS and Android mobile devices. There is also a companion website where users can login to see the webpages they have saved. Pocket provides greater ease of use since it is integrated in over 300 other mobile applications, including Facebook, Twitter, and Google Reader.[18] Both Pocket and Instapaper mobile apps allow users to save practically anything they find online so that they can access and read the items at a later time.

Teaching librarians can use both apps for organizing course content. When an instructor comes across an article or video that he wants to use in class, he can simply save it to either Instapaper or Pocket and access it later. Librarians can also encourage students to use these apps when collecting sources of information for assignments.

Course management apps

Course management apps allow teaching librarians to interact with students and keep track of course activities, such as attendance. Two of the apps listed below allow teachers to share videos with their students, and one even allows librarians to create videos on the go. Another app allows for virtual student conferencing, while the final app helps teaching librarians keep track of student attendance.

Air Video

Air Video (*www.inmethod.com/air-video/index.html;jsessio nid=4B1A5F4BA6F0650C7EFEC8E4F9DE84BE*) allows users to stream any video to their Apple iOS mobile devices (iPhone, iPad, and iPod Touch). Air Video converts videos that are usually incompatible with these devices so users can still access them. The application costs about US$2.99 (£2) and is only available for Apple iOS mobile devices.

Teaching librarians and their students can use this mobile app to watch videos that they would otherwise be unable to view on their Apple iOS mobile devices. Teachers who use a lot of videos in class can load the app on to class-designated iPads to have students view the assigned materials.

Attendance2

Attendance2 (*www.dave256apps.com/attendance/*) was created by an educator specifically for other educators. It allows teaching librarians to take class attendance and keep track of all attendance records. Instructors simply enter in the names of all their students for each course to start recording attendance statistics. Instructors can arrange students alphabetically by name or according to a specific seating chart. They can also attach photos to students' names, which helps in learning each name. Teaching librarians can use this app to mark students who are absent, present, late, or excused, or customize their own statuses.[19] Instructors can also store notes for each class and back up all the data collected from the app to a Dropbox account. Additionally, teachers can use the Attendance2 app to email their students directly from the app. It also allows teaching librarians to email themselves attendance reports and records for a given day or time period. Attendance2 was designed to run on Apple iOS mobile devices and costs about US$4.99 (£3). Teaching librarians who do not have Apple iOS devices or do not wish to pay for an attendance app should consider searching for similar products that are available in mobile app stores.

Qik

The Qik (*http://qik.com*) mobile app is available for both Apple iOS and Android mobile devices. The app is free for users, but there is also a Premium account that costs about

US\$4.99 (£3) per month or \$44.99 (£30) per year.[20] The Qik app allows users to capture and share videos using their mobile phones. Users have the option to share the videos live or at a later time. Users can easily share their videos via email or through many social networks such as Facebook, Twitter, and YouTube. Qik Premium allows users to sync videos on their mobile devices to their desktop computers. The Premium account also gives users unlimited video storage and the ability to record videos in high definition and 3D (as long as their devices support those features).

Teaching librarians can use this app to record lectures from any location and then share the lectures live with their students. This makes distant education easier, since all the librarian needs is a mobile device with a camera and an internet connection. Instructors can also use Qik to record class presentations or lectures so that students can access those videos at a later time. For example, a teacher could have students present projects and record the presentation. Students could then watch all the class presentations and critique and analyze their peers' presentation styles and the projects themselves. This is a great tool for collaboration and to help foster students' analytical and evaluative skills.

Skype

Skype (*www.skype.com/en/*) is a desktop application that allows users to video-chat with other Skype users in any location. Users need only a computer, a web camera, and a microphone to use the service. The basic version is free, but users can upgrade to a premium version to access features such as videoconferencing, sending text messages, and calling mobile phones and landlines. Premium accounts start at around US$4.99 (£3) per month.[21] Skype offers users free companion mobile applications for both Apple iOS and Android devices. Users of the Skype application simply utilize their mobile device's built-in camera and microphone to video-chat with other Skype users.

This desktop application and its companion mobile apps are great tools for teaching librarians, who can use them to set up student conferences when either the instructor or the student may be in a different location. Teachers can also use Skype applications for distance education, so long as a premium account is purchased, which allows for group conference video-chatting.

App builders

In addition to the useful mobile apps described above, there are many apps and tools that allow individuals to build their own customized mobile applications. Teaching librarians may be interested in creating custom course mobile apps where they can provide quick access to course documents such as the syllabus and assignments, course calendar, contact information, and even student grades. A custom application allows librarians to control the information in the app and gives them greater flexibility in how to use the app. It may also help protect sensitive information like student grades or other personal data. It allows teachers to offer a great course tool at no additional cost to their students, and to choose whether the app will be supported on both Apple iOS and Android devices. A course-specific mobile app allows students to access course materials from anywhere as long as they have access to a mobile device.

A quick internet search for 'app builder' is all it takes to find a reputable tool. Examples include BuildAnApp (*www.buildanapp.com/home*) and MyAppBuilder (*http://myappbuilder.com*), both of which allow users to create mobile applications that run on Apple iOS and Android devices. Both BuildAnApp and MyAppBuilder charge a fee to use their services, ranging from US$19 to $499 (£12–£329) depending on the services and features used.

Considerations: cost, security and privacy, availability, and reliability

Prior to using any mobile apps in their instruction, teaching librarians should carefully consider the following issues. First, while many educational mobile apps are free, many cost money to download and use on mobile devices. Teachers must decide whether the benefits of using a particular mobile app outweigh the costs of implementation. Librarians also must figure out who is going to cover the cost of a particular mobile app: the institution, the instructor, or the student. Some students may not be able to afford any additional costs associated with using mobile apps; and some institutions may not be willing or able to cover the costs of downloading and using the apps. Many applications have basic versions offered for free and premium or advanced versions at additional costs. Teaching librarians need to determine whether free versions offer all the tools they are interested in or if they need to purchase the premium versions.

Similar to cloud computing services, mobile apps come with inherent privacy and security risks. Information created and manipulated in mobile apps is typically stored remotely by a third party, usually the creator of the application. Because the information is stored remotely, the creators of the information (the teaching librarians or students) stored in a particular application cannot ensure that it is secure and remains private; instead, they must rely on third parties to protect it. Teaching librarians must keep this in mind and consider whether they want to entrust their course materials and student assignments to third-party providers. Content can also be lost in a variety of ways, from elaborate hacking operations to basic app malfunction. Many mobile apps have safeguards in place, and teachers should read the security and privacy policies for each mobile app they intend to use. Even with these safeguards, due to security and privacy concerns, librarians may need to get approval from their institutions prior to using mobile apps in their instruction. Some institutions may have policies in place discouraging the use of these applications due to student privacy concerns.

If a teaching librarian implements a specific mobile app as a main component of his course, that app must be reliable. Teachers should carefully read any available user reviews of mobile apps to see if there are major or minor reliability or security issues. They should also research the creator of a specific app to determine whether the app is likely to be reliable and secure. Since most mobile apps are maintained and updated by third-party providers, teaching librarians have no control over when features are updated or app maintenance is performed. Just as with cloud computing services, any updates or maintenance to mobile apps may cause certain features or even the entire service to be unavailable to users for an extended period of time. This could negatively impact students' use and perception of the app, which could in turn result in poor participation. If students or teaching librarians need to update constantly to newer versions of apps, they may not want to continue using them.

Not all mobile apps are available on all devices. Teaching librarians must take this into consideration when choosing which apps to include in instruction. It may be a good idea to poll students in class to see which devices most own or have access to. Due to the fact that not all students may have access to mobile devices with which to use educational mobile apps, teaching librarians should also see if their institution provides mobile devices, such as tablets, for classroom use. If so, they should see how many are available and find out if there are any policies in place for what they can and cannot add to the devices.

A final point of consideration for those wishing to use mobile apps in their instruction is training users on the devices. Because mobile apps are so prevalent in today's society, many students and instructors will require little to no training. However, some librarians and even some students (especially non-traditional students) may need training on how properly to use all the interactive and collaborative features available to them. Librarians need to consider whether the benefits of using a particular mobile app outweigh the time it takes to set up, maintain, and train themselves and their students on the use of the service.

In conclusion, prior to using any of these mobile apps, teaching librarians should carefully consider the following issues.

- Consider costs associated with each mobile app that will be used in pedagogy and who will pay for the apps.

- Be aware that the materials stored on mobile apps are at risk for security and privacy breaches, and users must rely on third parties to ensure the security of their documents.

- Keep in mind that not all mobile apps provide the same level of reliability, and things such as maintenance and updates are out of teachers' control, therefore carefully read user reviews and determine the reliability of both the app itself and its creator.

- Ensure students have access to mobile devices and educational mobile apps outside of the class or library.

- Consider the amount of training needed by all users prior to using a particular mobile app.

Best practices for using mobile apps in pedagogy

Teaching librarians who want to use mobile apps in their instruction should note the following best practices. First, as with any new course activity, teachers should consider conducting a pilot study on using a specific mobile app. For example, a teaching librarian who wants her students to use Trello to assist with group project management could solicit colleagues to try out the app prior to using it in class. This would allow her to ensure all content on the app functions properly, including assigning tasks to different group members, adding checklists, and adding due dates, prior to allowing her students to view and interact with the mobile app in and out of class. As another example, a teaching librarian who wants to use Qik to create and share instructional videos with her students should try creating a few videos on the fly to ensure her device's camera works properly. She should then try sharing the videos via email or by uploading them to YouTube or another social networking site. Teachers should use the pilot to ensure not only content works properly, but also the mobile app is user friendly. The pilot study can help teaching librarians identify any areas that may require additional training for users, especially non-traditional students. For more detailed information on conducting a pilot study, see Chapter 5.

Since not all students have access to mobile devices, instructors may want to consider having a certain number of devices, such as tablets, available for student use. These could be preloaded with the educational apps that the instructor wants her students to use for various course assignments and activities. Having the mobile apps preloaded to the devices allows the teaching librarian to ensure that the apps run properly and carry out the tasks intended. If the institution provides mobile devices to students for in-class use, teachers need to be sure to follow all institutional policies for using the devices, including what types of apps they can and cannot load to the device and use in class.

Teaching librarians should post clearly stated policies on proper student use and behavior when contributing content to interactive mobile apps. Specifically, they should inform their students about what is and is not proper to post to group projects and assignments, remind students about plagiarism, and instruct them on the basics of copyright infringement. Teaching librarians should monitor all student activity on the mobile apps and remind students that just because an app may seem informal, it is still being used in the course of formal instruction, so mobile devices and apps should be used in an appropriate manner. Teachers may want to consider deducting class points for repeat violations of any of the stated policies.

Students are not the only users who must be mindful of copyright laws; teaching librarians must obtain permission from students for future use of the information and materials they contribute to collaborative mobile apps, such as Trello and Inspiration Maps. Librarians must also be careful not to link to or embed outside sources that contain infringing material. For a more detailed look at copyright laws in the United States and the United Kingdom, see Chapter 6.

Teaching librarians can implement mobile apps to encourage students to collaborate and interact with their peers by sharing rich information with each other, such as videos, audio files, and links to outside sources. They should also encourage students not just to receive this information passively, but to be critical of it and constructively evaluate their peers' contributions to group assignments. Many of the apps listed in the previous sections foster creativity, collaboration, and evaluation, and teaching librarians should take advantage of those features.

In conclusion, teaching librarians should consider the following best practices prior to using mobile apps in their instruction.

- Conduct a pilot study for specific mobile apps to ensure all features function properly and identify areas that require additional user training.

- Consider providing mobile devices with preloaded educational mobile apps that students can access both in and out of class, but be sure to follow all institutional policies on use of shared mobile devices.

- Post policies on proper student use and behavior when contributing content to mobile apps, including information about plagiarism and the basics of copyright infringement.

- Monitor student activity and deduct points for repeat violations of course policies.

- Be mindful of the copyright implications of their own contributions to mobile apps.

- Encourage collaboration and critical thinking by allowing students to evaluate their peers' contributions to group projects created with mobile apps.

Conclusion

Mobile apps offer teaching librarians many ways to improve their instruction: they foster use of educational Web 2.0 tools, facilitate student and instructor interactivity, make distance education easier to conduct, and allow access to and editing of course documents from practically any location.

There are thousands of mobile apps available to teaching librarians and students. Teachers should take some time to research the best apps for their needs and start using them both for course organization and in their instruction.

While mobile apps offer many benefits to librarians and their students, they also come with risk. These risks include security and privacy breaches, ease of use and cost of access for students and instructors, reliability, and availability across devices. Teaching librarians must carefully weigh the risks and benefits of mobile applications before deciding to use them in their instruction.

Notes

1. Aquino, Carmela (2013) 'Digital future in focus series'; available at: *www.comscore.com/Insights/Blog/2013_Digital_Future_in_Focus_Series* (accessed: 15 February 2013).
2. Brophy, Keith (2013) 'Can you ignore billions of downloaded mobile apps?', 24 January; available at: *www.grbj.com/blogs/4-technology/post/76001-can-you-ignore-billions-of-downloaded-mobile-apps* (accessed: 15 February 2013).
3. Young, J. (2011) '6 top smartphone apps to improve teaching, research, and your life: academics describe going mobile to plan lectures, keep up with scholarship, and run classes', *Chronicle of Higher Education*, January; available at: *http://chronicle.com/article/6-Top-Smartphone-Apps-to/125764/*

(accessed: 12 February 2013); Walker, T. (2011) 'Get smart! Using mobile apps to improve your teaching', National Education Association; available at: *www.nea.org/home/41992.htm* (accessed: 12 February 2013); Le, R. and Duffy, T. (2012) '50 great apps for librarians'; available at: *http://50apps.weebly.com* (accessed: 12 February 2013).

4. Schroeder, B. (2010) '10 ways to use the iPad in your classroom', April; available at: *http://edtechtoday.wordpress.com/2010/04/23/ipad-2/* (accessed: 12 February 2013).

5. Johnston, H. and Stoll, C. (2011) 'It's the pedagogy, stupid: lessons from an iPad lending program', *eLearn Magazine*, May; available at: *http://elearnmag.acm.org/featured.cfm?aid=1999656* (accessed: 12 February 2013).

6. Franklin, T. (2011) 'Mobile learning: at the tipping point', *Turkish Online Journal of Educational Technology*, 10(4): 261–75.

7. Boopsie, 'Boopsie for libraries'; available at: *www.boopsie.com/library/* (accessed: 14 February 2013).

8. Boopsie, 'Standard package'; available at: *www.boopsie.com/library/products/standard-package/* (accessed: 14 February 2013).

9. Boopsie, 'Optimum package'; available at: *www.boopsie.com/library/products/optimum-package/* (accessed: 14 February 2013).

10. 'Library Anywhere'; available at: *www.libanywhere.com* (accessed: 14 February 2013).

11. Catch, 'Pricing'; available at: *https://catch.com/learn-more/pricing/* (accessed: 14 February 2013).

12. Catch, 'About'; available at: *https://catch.com/learn-more/why/* (accessed: 14 February 2013).

13. Evernote, 'Premium'; available at: *http://evernote.com/premium/* (accessed: 13 February 2013).

14. iTunes, 'Inspiration Maps'; available at: *https://itunes.apple.com/us/app/inspiration-maps/id510173686?mt=8* (accessed: 13 February 2013).

15. 'EasyBib'; available at: *www.easybib.com/kb/index/view/id/119* (accessed: 14 February 2013).

16. Trello, 'Tour'; available at: *https://trello.com/tour* (accessed: 13 February 2013).

17. iTunes, 'Article Search'; available at: *https://itunes.apple.com/us/app/articlesearch/id401914624?mt=8* (accessed: 14 February 2013).

18. 'Pocket'; available at: *http://getpocket.com/apps/* (accessed: 14 February 2013).

19. 'Attendance'; available at: *www.dave256apps.com/attendance/* (accessed: 14 February 2013).

20. Qik, 'Premium'; available at: *http://qik.com/info/premium* (accessed: 13 February 2013).

21. Skype, 'Premium'; available at: *www.skype.com/en/premium/* (accessed: 13 February 2013).

5

Preparing faculty, administration, and students for Web 2.0 tools, and an introduction to Web 3.0

Abstract: This chapter discusses ways to obtain approval from academy administration to utilize Web 2.0 and 3.0 tools in pedagogy. It conveys techniques to retain such approval and prevent, discover, and fix technological hitches that arise in using Web 2.0 tools, while constantly improving the implementation of Web 2.0 and 3.0 tools in pedagogy. Methods used in these tasks include pre-test/post-test endeavors, comment boxes, proper training for teaching librarians, and recruiting students for pilot studies. The chapter discusses emerging Web 3.0 technologies such as affective computing software, augmented reality, and holograms that will soon be utilized by teaching librarians.

Key words: Web 2.0, Web 3.0, comment box, pre-test/post-test, administrative approval, teaching librarian confidence, augmented reality, affective computing software, holograms.

Introduction – preparing the faculty for the technological revolution

Two omnipresent mammoth barriers to utilizing Web 2.0 tools are the lack of success in obtaining university administrative support and acceptance of the tools, and gaining librarian comfort with using Web 2.0 tools for pedagogical purposes. Successfully acquiring support requires conveying and displaying to academy administration that teaching librarians are equipped with the necessary knowledge to implement these technologies successfully with self-confidence. For teaching librarians to gain psychological attributes such as self-confidence they must feel comfortable utilizing Web 2.0 tools without fear. Unfortunately, a fear of using these tools is more common for teaching librarians than is self-confidence. Ho et al.[1] experimented with using Second Life in the classroom to offer students a richer context in which to learn materials. However, their results revealed that using the technology led to several in-class technical glitches. These technological malfunctions can exacerbate fear and ultimately lead to complete avoidance of Web 2.0 tools among teaching librarians, and may have deleterious educational consequences for students. Technological glitches must be prevented as much as possible, and for those impossible to prevent, teachers must be properly trained so they are comfortable in dealing with the glitches when utilizing Web 2.0 tools. Proper training and practice that implements techniques to avoid technological problems or resolve any hitches that arise can also prevent in-class embarrassment in front of students. Being equipped with such preventive and solution-oriented tools can ultimately lead to greater acceptance of Web 2.0 tools by teaching librarians, and subsequently school administration support as well.

Methods to alleviate fear and reduce technology glitches

Many methods exist to assuage the reticence of librarians' usage and administrations' adoption of Web 2.0 tools.

For example, to reduce educators' anxiety, Ho et al. recommend faculty complete a pilot study using Web 2.0 technology prior to utilizing it in class. This pilot study could reveal common technological malfunctions and learning curves, help educators know how to deal efficiently and effectively with these problems in-class, and not deleteriously affect student learning since the glitches are discovered during a pilot. Such a study could also alleviate concerns and fears teaching librarians may have about interacting with Web 2.0 tools.[2]

How would a pilot study be carried out?

A pilot study could be implemented in a number of ways that would not be detrimental to student grades or learning.

- Recruit current undergraduate or graduate students to participate in a grant-funded summer experiment to test using a Web 2.0 tool.

- After completing a pilot, use this Web 2.0 tool live in a subsequent semester.

- Implement the pilot study during a pass/fail class with clear disclosure given to students prior to commencement that this is an experimental course in which the educational benefits will consist of learning how to use a Web 2.0 tool/tools, discovering how to manage technology problems, and ascertaining new knowledge in a substantive area. For example, in a hospital administration class students could learn how to use a wiki to organize, share, and critique financial data. In concert with learning how to use these data, students could discover how to use a wiki, how to manage technological hitches that arise with the wiki, and how to solve those glitches.

- Emphasize that student grades are not negatively affected by technological glitches, or how those glitches are managed.

- Provide an interactive feedback forum in the Web 2.0 tool. Provide clear instructions to students as where to locate the forum, where to access it, how to submit or save comments, and how to edit comments.

- In the interactive forum, encourage students to express what they like, dislike, and experienced frustration with, and how they managed any frustrations, barriers, or specific technological anomalies.

- Provide in-class training to faculty and students during this pilot study.

Example – pilot study

Research completed by Ellison and Matthews[3] exemplified how to test a Web 2.0 technology in a pilot study. The researchers implemented a two-step process in which they first offered students course credit to investigate a property in Second Life and submit a proposal to build it. Next, if the proposal was approved by the instructor, the students built the learning site as a rendition that would coincide with the relevant substantive area of pedagogy. Such a study could be set up in any educational context (junior high, high school, college, graduate school) and allow students to earn course credit by participating in the careful and detailed planning and a trial-and-error pilot phase of a Web 2.0 tool such as a wiki. During this pilot phase, teaching librarians and students would be sleuthing for any potential technological problems. Simultaneously, the course would inculcate substantive knowledge to students pertinent to whatever subject was being studied. The course could be offered for one or two academic terms. If possible, having the same students for two consecutive terms may produce rich information regarding what technological malfunctions occur and how to manage them, and give different perspectives on each of these two areas. Thus, for example, a teacher could offer a business research management one and an advanced business research management two class in consecutive academic terms to encourage students to enroll in successive terms. Such uninterrupted enrollment could help perfect the use of Web 2.0 tools for pedagogical purposes.

Many pedagogical areas could replicate this pilot study for course credit. For example, hospital management students at the undergraduate level could receive course credit by initially investigating an area in Second Life, proposing a pedagogical venue, and setting it up while learning about substantive issues related to this field of study. Students putting the proposal together would have to consider potential environmental threats to a new hospital location, economics, corporate structure, politics between doctors, nurses, administrators, and staff, where to build the hospital café and gift store... While thinking critically about these issues, discerning whether their own ideas are valid, and synthesizing new suggestions, the students are discovering potential technological threats and learning how to deal with them. Teaching librarians in turn can use this learned knowledge in future academic terms and continue to improve the virtual educational venue once it is established.

Managing the technical glitches – an example involving feedback

Another way to implement a Web 2.0 tool successfully and manage its technological hitches is to develop one's own virtual teaching space and solicit peer review regarding its ease of use, usability, barriers to learning, technological complications, and other ramifications. Lancaster University Law School in the United Kingdom did just that, offering a training program for faculty and students before it implemented a virtual learning space called the LUVLE.[4] This program had a feedback forum requesting comments about the user friendliness of the technology and recommendations as to how to make the site a better learning tool, and emphasizing that technology should never be implemented for its own sake, but should be tweaked to benefit the high-level learning of students.[5]

A teaching librarian who creates a similar pilot program can learn about any potential technological glitches, discover solutions regarding how to fix these malfunctions, and thus ultimately provide a better product for teaching staff and students after the program is completed. Some of the potential benefits garnered by students and librarians via a pilot are as follows.

- Librarians and other faculty may not be as fearful of using a virtual space if they participate in the pilot because they develop a sense of ownership and comfort.

- Students and faculty learn how to anticipate, detect, and effectively deal with technological glitches.

- Administration becomes cognizant that not all technological glitches produce negative outcomes. To the contrary, some glitches may present learning opportunities for students and teaching librarians as they develop tools to recognize and deal with these malfunctions. Further, such glitches offer opportunities to improve and tweak virtual learning environments.

- Students will be presented with technological glitches in the work world after they graduate, thus allowing them to attempt to solve technology problems in an academy prepares them well for their future professional endeavors.

- As this virtual product is utilized in successive academic terms, the system is improved, faculty and students become more adept at using it, and hopefully it improves student learning.

Teaching librarians should continuously monitor whether such a virtual teaching tool is improving student learning. They may do so by implementing pre-test/post-test evaluations.

- Use an essay format at the beginning and end of each academic term to measure student learning.

- Utilize a Likert-type survey at the beginning and end of each term to discover whether adequate student learning has occurred.

- Implement an oral evaluation at the beginning and end of each term to establish whether student learning has improved.

- Have students complete a brief hands-on activity at the beginning and end of each term.

- Conduct a student focus group at the beginning and end of each term.

- Complete a dependent group t-test using SPSS to determine whether the use of a Web 2.0 tool has produced increased student learning.

How to implement a pre-test/post-test to evaluate a Web 2.0 tool continually

To ensure continued pedagogical benefits from the utilization of Web 2.0 tools, teaching librarians should use some type of measurement that deciphers whether the tool is increasing, decreasing, or having no effect on student learning. A pre-test/post-test format is a method that can be applied to measure the effect on student learning. For example, suppose a librarian is teaching a class on business management, and wants to use a Mindomo to help convey how encouraging creativity benefits employee performance. A pre-test/post-test measurement could be utilized to evaluate learning. The procedure involves having students fill out a short questionnaire prior to commencement of the lesson. After imparting knowledge and giving students an opportunity to express their learned information by building Mindomo maps, critically review their peers' thinking maps, and synthesize new knowledge via the Mindomo maps, the librarian then gives the students a similar questionnaire that elicits the exact same information prompted in the pre-test. If the post-test indicates higher scores than did the pre-test, this may be indicative that the Mindomo augmented student learning. Educators should continue to track student progress each academic term to evaluate consistently whether Mindomo, or any other Web 2.0 tool, is increasing learning. That said, one could argue that the test-retest component of this type of method, or some other confounding variable, is responsible for increased student learning. However, if learning is continuously increasing from pre-test to post-test each academic term, that is the goal of effective pedagogy, and therefore one may wish to continue to use a Mindomo, or whichever Web 2.0 tool is chosen. If the pre-test/post-test design suggests student learning is decreasing, the educator may want to utilize other Web 2.0 tools to enhance learning. Other pre-test/post-test measures include the following.

- Have students write a one-page essay pre- and post-instruction.

- Have students create a project or task in a digital environment pre- and post-instruction.

- Require students to complete a survey pre- and post-instruction.

- Request students to complete research tasks pre- and post-instruction.

- Perform an oral evaluation of a pre- and post-instruction task for students.

- Conduct a student focus group at the beginning and end of each academic term.

- Complete a dependent samples *t*-test with a standardized questionnaire to decipher whether student learning is increasing as a result of using a Web 2.0 tool in pedagogy.

Practical use of this empirical knowledge

The empirical research referenced above suggests these important concepts.

- Do not use technology for technology's sake, instead only use technology that will enhance an educator's ability to stimulate student interest in a substantive topic, or will provide rich-text, deep-level learning environments.

- Help the students make connections from long-term memory to new content.

- Test technology before implementing it in a live classroom.

- Train educators to recognize and deal with technological glitches quickly and efficiently.

- Run a pre-test/post-test to discover whether a selected Web 2.0 tool is continuously improving student learning. Tests can be conducted using essay format, a questionnaire, an oral discussion, student focus groups, or dependent samples *t*-tests.

- Offer a comment forum for students and faculty; ensure the information technology department reads this forum and discusses all options with librarians, other instructors, and administrators.

Emerging technologies – Web 3.0

A panoply of horizon technologies endeavor to increase the ease with which librarians offer pedagogy. Such technologies further assist in developing confidence in teaching librarians and administration. These Web 3.0 technologies are not only dynamic and allow users to modify and actively interact with them, as do Web 2.0 tools, but also respond to users' perceived emotional needs. For example, some Web 3.0 technologies anticipate or sense a user's emotional and information needs. Others provide a two- or three-dimensional reality for users so they can view information that is impossible to view in Web 2.0 or Web 1.0 format. Some Web 3.0 content interacts via lasers where users can perceive things from different perspectives, based on where the user is physically located. These emerging technologies include affective computing software (ACS), augmented reality, and holograms.

Affective computing software

ACS is a horizon software that can independently detect a computer user's current emotional state. Thus the software can determine whether a computer user is satisfied or discontent with the current search results he or she is receiving when conducting research. The software is able to perceive a computer user's current affect via its augmented transition network (ATN). This network is basically a system of internal decision trees that determines whether to retrieve, maintain, or delete information located or stored on a computer based on the perceived effect on a computer user.[6] The ATN attempts to perceive the user's current emotions via physiological data, such as his or her heart rate, blood pressure, and galvanic skin response. These physiological symptoms are deciphered in embedded sensors in a computer mouse, a glove worn by the user, or some other embedded sensor.[7] ACS is also capable of detecting user dissatisfaction by recognizing universally known negative facial expressions, such as frowning or displaying anger or frustration. Researchers at Brunel University have shown that various facial conveyances of anger or frustration are displayed by the specific alignment of certain facial muscles.[8] ACS recognizes these alignments via a camera attached to a computer and interprets whether a computer user is frustrated or content. If ACS perceives the user as being content, then it continues to offer the sources located on the computer and may search for similar sources. If ACS interprets the user's physiological symptoms to convey frustration or unhappiness, it will recommend different sources or technical searches. The leading researcher in this area, Rosalind Picard, has successfully developed and implemented this software to help individuals with autism become more aware of their feelings.[9]

ACS *in pedagogy*

ACS may benefit pedagogy in the future in numerous guises, such as by serving as a teaching assistant. While teaching a large class, ACS can assist frustrated students when a librarian is not even aware a student is experiencing difficulty locating needed information. For example, if a librarian is instructing a class with 40 or more students, many of them are sure to be introverts and thus less likely to express dissatisfaction orally. Or perhaps a teacher is giving instruction in an online course format where he or she cannot even perceive the students' various emotions. ACS can detect current student satisfaction or dissatisfaction via a student's negative physiological symptoms, or his or her negative facial expressions. When ACS recognizes student distress, it can properly assist a student by suggesting pertinent websites based on student keyword searches, or relevant databases, articles, books, or other pertinent sources. Thus ACS assists a librarian who is offering instruction to many students, assists the librarian in helping those who need research help, and independently saves students time by quickly and efficiently offering them research assistance, perhaps even before the student realizes he or she needs help.

ACS can also benefit the librarian's pedagogical process by alerting him or her to students' particular learning styles. Each student learns best via kinesthetic, auditory, or visual stimulation, or some combination thereof. If a student frequently accesses videos via YouTube or some other video archive, this may indicate an auditory or visual learning preference. In contrast, if a student exhibits frustration when being directed to complete a mind map, it may indicate the student does not have a kinesthetic learning preference. ACS can succor a librarian in discovering these learning preferences. By becoming cognizant of preferences, librarians may provide appropriate learning tools such as Mindomos, challenges to solve in Second Life, or other manipulatives to kinesthetic learners; and YouTube videos, recorded MP3 lectures, and other auditory pedagogical stimulation to auditory learners. Thus ACS has the potential as a new Web 3.0 tool to augment pedagogy by helping librarians discover each student's preferred learning style, help and assist frustrated and content students, and then provide the appropriate learning tools.

Potential detriments of ACS

Misinterpretation of student physiological symptoms

One potential deleterious ramification of ACS is its possibility of misinterpreting a computer user's physiological symptoms. Even though facial recognition software has displayed success at determining a person's current affect, a user may show displeasure while completing research due to factors other than the sources he or she is retrieving on a computer.[10] For example, a student may be focused on the reality that he or she just broke up with a significant other, or thinking about frustrations experienced in another class, or reacting to a recent comment made by a fellow classmate. Any of these stimuli may cause elevated blood pressure, increased heart rate, varied galvanic skin response, or a facial conveyance of displeasure or frustration. ACS could easily misinterpret these physiological manifestations as a student being unhappy with current content displayed on a computer interface, which may cause it to begin recommending unrelated content, websites, databases, or articles. Such unwanted recommendations of irrelevant information will cause student frustration, and thus ACS can harm rather than help a teaching librarian's pedagogy.

Student privacy issues

Invasion of privacy is a concern in implementing ACS. For example, how many students will feel comfortable in allowing software to record, store, and interpret their physiological symptoms such as blood pressure, heart rate, and galvanic skin response? One could craft a valid argument that in recent years computer users have become desensitized to violations of privacy. Most students today probably post everything about their life on ubiquitous social forums such as Facebook, Twitter, and Google+. Information that was considered private ten years ago is now expected to be posted on Facebook 24 hours a day. Students constantly update what they are eating, with whom they are in a relationship, and their likes and dislikes. Further, contemporary students comfortably and willingly post revealing photos of themselves and their friends.

Despite such willingness to create revealing electronic dossiers, there is still some collective belief that posting one's medical records or physiological information online for all to see is taboo and embarrassing. People may question what a future employer would do with such information. Would someone not date me due to the revelation of an irregular heartbeat...? Therefore, as ACS records private physiological symptoms, it begs the question of whether this is a violation of privacy. Of course, since ACS is a horizon technology, courts in the United Kingdom, the United States, and other countries have not addressed this issue. However, privacy laws in various countries protect the disclosure of medical information without patient consent. Thus one would assume this would be a violation of UK law and US law, unless student assent was obtained.

Informed consent

ACS may breach the common notions of informed consent. Informed consent suggests that one is voluntarily agreeing to subject oneself to ACS, and has been completely informed about all of the possible known negative ramifications of assenting to such use of a technology, and precisely how the technology works.[11] Thus a librarian would need to give a student a written statement describing how ACS works, the type of information it would be sensing, storing, and evaluating, and its possible known deleterious ramifications, and conveying that the student does not have to submit to the technology. Then the student could make an informed decision as to whether he or she wanted to assent to ACS.

Would positional power affect a student's decision?

One must question whether a student would resist using a computer equipped with ACS when asked by a teaching librarian to do so. Most students would probably acquiesce simply because someone of higher authority was asking them to do research on an ACS-enabled computer. Students in general are likely to consent to instructor direction or request due to their perception of a faculty member (librarian) having a superior position of power. The student is likely to be placed in a situation where he or she feels vulnerable to the librarian due to his or her positional power, trusts and relies on the librarian, and so complies with the direction to use a computer equipped with ACS.[12] A student forms this perception of an inferior position of bargaining power due to being cognizant that the librarian is assigning the student's ultimate grade. Thus a student is less likely to protest about using an ACS-enabled computer even if the librarian explains what personal data ACS records, how it stores them, and for what these data may be used. Because of the chasm in positional power, if a student acquiesces to completing research on a computer equipped with ACS, has he or she really given voluntary consent? Or has the imbalance in positional power forced consent? If so, may a teaching librarian ethically utilize the data gathered from the student's search process? Or is this a form of unintended coercion?

Augmented reality

Augmented reality is an emerging Web 3.0 tool that may be utilized by teaching librarians. Augmented reality is different from virtual reality, which presents an interface that simulates the real word, like Second Life, an airplane simulator, or a skiing simulator. In contrast, augmented reality displays a segment of the real world while draping over additional information.[13] For example, an augmented reality interface may show a depiction of a real human body with an overlay of human organs, muscle tissue, bones, or circulatory systems.

Pedagogical uses of augmented reality

Teaching librarians could use augmented reality to assist in giving reference instruction to junior high, high school, undergraduate, or graduate-level students. For example, a librarian could obtain copyright permission or utilize a statutory copyright exception to show contemporary music videos as a mashup via YouTube, and while displaying the videos depict an overlay of bibliographic information on the screen. Bibliographic information could consist of the artist's name, song title, publisher... of the various songs compiled in the mashup. All this information could initially appear jumbled as each song is illustrated; then all bibliographic details could come together at the end to form a concise and correct citation. Such pedagogical Web 2.0 (YouTube) and Web 3.0 (augmented reality) tools attract the attention of students, and in turn this teaches them a valuable lesson – how to cite information properly.

A librarian may also use augmented reality while teaching a substantive topic such as law. For example, when attempting to convey visual examples to students of the various thousands of documents contained in a specific legal database, often a librarian must click through ten, 20, or more electronic pages to display some of the different content. However, with augmented reality, the librarian may remain on a database's homepage throughout his or her entire soliloquy, and use augmented reality to display hundreds of documents in the database. A teacher could visually depict how a database contains legal statutes, cases, regulations, articles, treatises, encyclopedias... all without ever leaving the displayed database's homepage. Thus the augmented reality tool prevents distracting clicking from page to page, prevents a librarian from getting lost in his or her instruction, and alleviates boredom for students, at least theoretically.

Holograms

A hologram is a projection of a pre-recorded three-dimensional image. This projection is created using a laser, and the perception of the projected image varies depending upon the angle from which it is being viewed. Thus viewing a hologram is similar to viewing a tangible object in front of you. For example, when looking at a multicolored beach ball, depending on where one is standing, a person may declare the ball is red and white. However, someone standing on the other side of the ball may say that it is blue and yellow. As these two individuals walk around the ball they will see that many colors are depicted on the ball. Holograms project and create similar perceptions. Thus a person looking at an image of a multicolored brick building projected by a hologram may have a similar experience of perceiving that the building is only one color when viewing it from only one angle. Yet viewing the projection from alternate angles, he or she sees many different colors displayed on the building. The movie *Star Wars* popularized holograms, as they were depicted as a communication device in parts four, five, and six of the series. At the time theaters showed *Star Wars* movies, most of the public assumed such a device was as far-fetched as a time machine. However, the utilization of holograms is now an emerging technology and ripe to be used in pedagogical endeavors.

Use of holograms in French airports

Orly Airport in Paris, France, uses holograms to project 2D images of boarding agents which convey general information to passengers as they are boarding a plane. The image is projected on to a human-shaped piece of Plexiglas. Such an anthropomorphic depiction could catalyze frustration and dissent among travelers with specific questions, but one must assume that Orly Airport continues to offer human agents who will answer such questions. Reports regarding these French transit-related holograms indicate the majority of travelers receive them well, and children especially show great interest in the projections.[14]

Holograms in pedagogy

Holograms could be used to benefit pedagogy in a variety of guises. A teaching librarian could implement holograms to give instruction regarding any substantive area by recording lectures, demonstrations, or brief comments for students to view outside of the classroom. Having access to such holographic projections benefits students because they are allowed to view these lectures, comments, demonstrations... at their leisure; they have a holographic archive to which they may refer while preparing to write a term paper or studying for an exam; and they may consult a demonstration (e.g. how to operate on a cadaver, how to look up content in a database, how to convey non-verbal communication while giving a speech) when attempting to complete a kinesthetic task or practicing an auditory task. Thus when offering instruction in an all-online format, holograms conveniently serve as a supplemental tool with which students may access further instruction. When instructing in a face-to-face or hybrid format, librarians may also offer holographic recordings to students to view before class so they arrive prepared and eager to perform hands-on tasks. Or holographic projections may serve as an out-of-class educational archive. Alternatively, if a teacher cannot attend a class session, students could view the projection of a lecture via a hologram. By still having students present, they openly discuss confusing issues and complete hands-on tasks or other class projects.

As mentioned above, the children in Orly Airport showed great interest in the airport holograms.[15] Castillo[16] additionally noted that kids find photonics such as lasers, optics, and fiber optics interesting. This emerging technology catches their attention. Perhaps this is why the popularity of the *Star Wars* movies appears to be perpetual. Ergo, this emerging technology creates a rich-text, hands-on learning environment that kids (ages one to 99) get excited about: they are eager to pay attention to the content being iterated, and thus they are more likely to retain said content cognitively. Kids in this context include pupils in kindergarten through graduate school.

Pedagogical exercises using holograms

Many outdoor artistic depictions are created with paint or projected light, and sunlight often dilutes these works. However, using holographic projections to create the same art on buildings or other structures produces more homogeneous coloring and preserves the intended color of the artistic depiction,[17] due to a hologram projection's ability to absorb sunlight. Thus a teaching librarian could use holograms to juxtapose how different light (e.g. fluorescent, sunlight…) affects the desired depiction of color. Holograms could be used with architectural students, art pupils, or in some types of course addressing environmental concerns. While using a hologram, a librarian could tie in how to give proper citation to the creators of specific artistic techniques; books, articles, or websites addressing these techniques; and videos conveying the techniques. Teaching librarians could further use holograms to record demonstrations on how to use specific databases, how to search for reliable and valid information with a web browser, or how to avoid copyright infringement and plagiarism.

Conclusion

Teaching librarians need to spend time with Web 2.0 and Web 3.0 tools prior to using them. By doing so, they can illustrate to academy administration that they can utilize these tools without a negative effect on student learning. However, learning to use these tools can be a collaborative effort by inviting students to participate in pilot studies in which the librarian and student learn together how to predict, manage, and solve technological glitches involved with Web 2.0 and 3.0 tools. Providing course credit is a good motivator to attract willing students to help with such academic endeavors. Also, teachers must anticipate the need to continue to be flexible and willing to learn new pedagogical tools with the emergence of Web 3.0 technologies such as affective computing software, holograms, and augmented reality. In short, utilizing these tools can catch the attention of students, engage their inquisitive nature, and be a positive learning experience for students and teaching librarians.

Notes

1. Ho, C.M.L., Rappa, N.A., and Chee, Y.S. (2009) 'Designing and implementing virtual enactive role-play and structured argumentation: promises and pitfalls', *Computer Assisted Language Learning*, 22(5): 381.
2. Ibid.
3. Ellison, K. and Matthews, C. (2010) 'Virtual history: a socially networked pedagogy of enlightenment', *Educational Research*, 57(3): 297–307.
4. Bloxham, S. and Armitage, S. (2003) 'What a LUVLE way to learn law', *International Review of Law, Computers & Technology*, 17(1): 39–50; available at: *www.tandf.co.uk/journals/cirl* (accessed: 15 February 2013).
5. Ibid.
6. Davis, B. (2005) 'Tell Laura I love her', *New Scientist*, 188: 42–6.
7. Helge, K. (2009) 'Emotional intelligence: the possibilities and pitfalls of affective computing software', *AALL Spectrum*, 14(3): 14–17.

8. Califf, S. (2003) 'Letting your computer know how you feel', *Computer Weekly*, 22: 2–5.

9. Picard, R.W. (2000) 'Toward computers that recognize and respond to user emotion', *IBM Systems Journal*, 39: 705–19.

10. Califf, note 8 above.

11. Reynolds, C. and Picard, R.W. (2004) 'Ethical evaluation of display that adapts to affect', *Cyber Psychology & Behavior*, 7: 662–6.

12. Toben, B. and Helge, K. (2012) 'Sexual misconduct with congregants or parishioners: crafting a model statute', *British Journal of American Legal Studies*, 1: 189–215.

13. Shneiderman, B. and Plaisant, C. (2010) *Designing the User Interface: Strategies for Effective Human-Computer Interaction*, 5th edn. Boston, MA: Pearson.

14. Tarantola, A. (2011) 'Paris airport gets holographic boarding agents', *Gizmodo*, 18 August; available at: *http://gizmodo.com/5832303/paris-airport-gets-holographic-boarding-agents* (accessed: 21 February 2013).

15. Ibid.

16. Castillo, R. (2000) 'Bringing holograms and laser light shows to science class', *Christian Science Monitor*, 15 August, p. 16.

17. Bakowska, M. (2007) 'Images in architecture – from murals to illuminating projections', *Town Planning and Architecture*, 31(1): 54–61.

6

Legal information related to Web 2.0 and Web 3.0

Abstract: This chapter discusses the possible legal pitfalls into which teaching librarians may fall if they use or allow the use of Web 2.0 and 3.0 tools in a negligent manner. Such pitfalls consist of defamation, copyright infringement, and the high cost of litigation. To avoid these, librarians should become aware generally of current laws in their jurisdiction, apply this knowledge of the law in their pedagogical endeavors, and inculcate their colleagues and students with such knowledge. The chapter additionally covers the application of Creative Commons licenses and the SPARC Addendum, both which allow for the wider usage and dissemination of copyrighted materials.

Key words: defamation, slander, libel, copyright, cost of litigation, Creative Commons, SPARC Addendum.

Introduction

Today's students, teaching librarians, and academy administration need to be cognizant of the possible legal ramifications of negligent or intentional postings that may disparage others, infringe copyright, or otherwise skirt the law. Students especially often post material or statements on Facebook, Google+, Twitter, and other Web 2.0 venues without putting much thought into the possible negative results. Usually nothing happens when such posts are made, but occasionally someone will face negative legal consequences when he or she negligently or intentionally posts something that is infringing or defamatory, or violates another's privacy.

US defamation

Defamation in the United States exists as either slander or libel, and is classified as a tort. Slander is generally defined as defamatory language expressed orally, whereas libel is usually defined as demeaning another in writing. In the United States there are many types of slander, such as slander *per se* and false-light slander. Further, each US state may have different statutory and judicial interpretations for separate types of defamation. The burden of proving one of these torts in American courts is placed on the plaintiff,[1] and this burden is quite high. However, with the increasing use of Web 2.0 and future rapid ascent of Web 3.0 tools in academies, university administrations, educators, and students need to be cognizant of the possible defamatory pitfalls into which they may fall as a result of staff, students, or faculty posting potentially libelous material to a blog, wiki, or some other Web 2.0 device. Further, recording videos with possible auditory and textual defamatory remarks and uploading them to an educational venue such as YouTube may result in potential liability for libel or slander.

Example of libel lawsuit in the United States

An example of a university being involved in a libel suit is two employees from the American Career College. One former college employee allegedly typed libelous information on Wikipedia about the college.[2] The ex-employee denied these allegations and filed a motion to dismiss, but a US district court allowed the case to move forward and be heard. This court noted that when considering a libel case, the courts must balance harm to the plaintiff against the First Amendment's right to free speech. A plaintiff's allegations 'must be enough to raise a right to relief above the speculative level'.[3] The speech must state a false fact, not merely an opinion.[4]

In this case, the specific libel suit consisted of a 'false-light claim', and the venue was an Illinois court. Under Illinois law, the plaintiff has to prove three elements to state a false-light claim: the plaintiff was placed in a false light before the public; a trier of fact could find the false light 'highly offensive to a reasonable person'; and the defendant acted with actual malice.[5] If this former employee is held liable for libelous statements about the college, a new precedent will be set, giving warning to employees, faculty, students, staff, and all academy members to be cognizant and wary of the information and opinions they post about colleges on Web 2.0 and 3.0 tools. All members of academies should be guided in their electronic postings by the adage of do not post anything on Facebook, Second Life, a website, or any other Web 2.0 tool that you do not want printed on the front page of a newspaper, or a website, or a blog... for the whole world to see! In the next section a student attending another university did not adhere to this adage, and as a result found himself in a precarious litigious situation.

A case at an American university

Students today are conditioned to accept perpetual postings of informal gossip and personal information about themselves or someone else, and sometimes inappropriate images on Facebook, Twitter, Google+, and other electronic venues. Although using these and other ubiquitous Web 2.0 and Web 3.0 tools in the classroom is pedagogically advantageous for the teaching librarian and the students, due to students' desensitization to posting personal information to public forums, academies must be cognizant of the potential legal pitfalls to which these tools expose students, faculty, staff, and members.

A case illustrative of what may happen if libelous postings are not prevented or immediately removed occurred at an academy in the United States. In 2009 this academy's administration discovered an anonymous blogger had posted some information in his blog that the administration interpreted to be defamatory toward the academy's reputation. The administration decided to sue the anonymous blogger. As it turned out, the blogger was a junior attending the plaintiff academy, thus the academy was suing one of its own students. This lawsuit challenges the standard of academic freedom of students, faculty, staff, and all members of academies set up by Chief Justice Earl Warren's comments in the case of *Sweezy v. New Hampshire*,[6] decided in 1957. Yet defamation lawsuits may become more common, pitting academy against student, staff, faculty, or other university member, with the increased use of Facebook, Twitter, online course software such as Blackboard, wikis, and other open source Web 2.0 tools. At a modicum, such behavior is likely to juxtapose academy member against academy member, which could easily cause strife in college camaraderie. This potential for divisive litigation encourages teaching librarians to advocate and create policies and guidelines that help deal with questionable student or faculty postings internally if possible.

Another recent lawsuit filed against a librarian in Canada

In another recent lawsuit, a librarian who worked for McMaster University in Ontario was sued by Edwin Mellon Press for material posted on a blog by the librarian at McMaster. Mellon Press alleged the information posted to the blog was libelous and sought more than $4 million in damages.[7] Mellon Press subsequently dropped the lawsuit. However, the fact this librarian was initially sued illustrates that one should be careful and cognizant about what content one posts to a blog to avoid potential litigation.

UK defamation

In the United Kingdom, a bill currently pending in Parliament potentially alters current defamation law by:

- requiring claimants to show serious harm before suing for defamation;

- disallowing a presumption for a jury trial;

- presenting a defense of 'responsible publication on matters of public interest' (some anticipate this may give journalists free rein to comment on any information, whether accurately corroborated by sources or not);

- providing extra protections to maintainers of websites;

- establishing new safe harbors if a defendant can prove truth or honest opinion.

This bill is posted in its full-text version on the UK Parliament website.[8]

Cost of litigation

Along with the divisiveness of litigation pitting academy against academy member, the cost of litigation for all involved is astronomical. For example, during a defamation case in Tarrant County, Texas, in the United States, a group of defendants were ordered by a jury to pay the plaintiff US$14 million (£8.7 million). In this case, plaintiffs had filed an internet libel suit against defendants alleging defamatory remarks were made on a blog. The verdict was overturned on appeal in a Tarrant County district court, yet the defendants were quoted as having to pay over $1 million (£623,000) in legal defense fees. So even though for now these defendants have avoided being held liable for libelous conduct and having to pay US$14 million to plaintiffs, they still have a $1 million attorneys' fee tab, filing costs, fees owed to expert witnesses, and other fees associated with litigation.[9] This holding could be overturned on appeal, and thus defendants still could be looking at a $14 million verdict against them. If a university was confronted with such a lawsuit, legal fees or a negative verdict could make a large dent in its endowment or legal reserve fund. Further, such lawsuits potentially damage the goodwill common between students, alumni, faculty, staff, administration, donors, and other members of the academy.

Although lawsuits against universities due to malevolent postings on blogs, wikis, and other Web 2.0 sites are not yet common, the increased use of these sites in pedagogy demands that university personnel become acquainted with current laws regarding slander and libel. Universities must create policies to prevent and quickly discover any vindictive or negligent Web 2.0 postings made by students, faculty, and staff; develop proper training that educates the university community regarding defamation; and provide efficient access to said policies. The following tips may assist academies in creating such policies.

- Appoint a scholarly communications librarian or scholarly communications officer to be in charge of staying abreast of laws regarding libel/slander.

- Provide training for staff, administration, and faculty in the dos and don'ts of posting on blogs, Facebook, and other Web 2.0 sites.

- Offer training for students educating them about the potential negative ramifications when posting inappropriate material to Web 2.0 or Web 3.0 venues.

- Pass along this training to students in class.

- Closely monitor student postings when using Web 2.0 tools in class.

- When inappropriate content is found, remove it quickly, but also use the situation as a teachable moment for faculty, administration, staff, and students.

- Deal with questionable faculty or student postings internally if possible.

- Create an internal retraining or judicial process to deal with violators of Web 2.0 postings policy.

- Create a centralized electronic site which faculty, staff, students, and administrators may consult to stay abreast of what are defamatory statements, how to avoid such comments, and how they may affect their pedagogical rights.

- On this centralized site, allow students, faculty, staff, and other academy members to post questions and comments that will be answered by the scholarly communications librarian or officer.

- Create and link videos to the academy webpage explaining what is and how to prevent defamation, copyright infringement, plagiarism, and violations of privacy, so students, faculty, staff, and the rest of the academy community have efficient access to this information.

Governmental immunity

Although many members of academies in the United Kingdom and the United States may argue that their electronic postings are protected by governmental immunity, with the evolving nature of defamation and copyright law due to Web 2.0 tools in most nations one may not wish to rely solely on such a defense. Additionally, for those teaching librarians and other academics who work for private entities, the safe harbor of governmental immunity is not available.

Copyright

Copyright is another legal pitfall into which teaching librarians may fall if they are not aware of current law, what is permissible, and what is considered legal taboo. Any time an instructor utilizes portions of articles, books, images, audio-visual material, sound recordings, musical renditions, or other creative works in pedagogy, he or she must be cognizant of the copyright laws that govern the particular work. This may mandate that the instructor be aware of copyright laws from different countries, as accessed scholarship is obtained from the United Kingdom, the United States, and other nation-states. Therefore, when using a portion of scholarship it is important to know which publisher produced the work to be certain one is complying with the correct country's copyright laws.

US copyright basics

Generally, when someone in the United States writes a book, article, poem, or other textual material, creates a webpage or course page, creates a painting, jots down notes on a napkin... or reduces any creation to tangible form they instantaneously receive the following basic copyrights:

- the sole right to reproduce said work
- the sole right to distribute said work
- the sole right to create a derivative of said work
- the sole right to perform said work
- the sole right to display said work.[10]

UK copyright basics

Copyright law in the United Kingdom commenced with the Statute of Anne in 1709.[11] The types of works protected under UK law consist of:

- literary – song lyrics, manuscripts, manuals, computer programs, commercial documents, leaflets, newsletters, articles etc.
- dramatic – plays and dances
- musical – recordings and scores
- artistic – photography, painting, sculptures, architecture, technical drawings/diagrams, maps, logos
- typographical arrangement of published editions – magazines, periodicals, etc.
- sound recording – recordings of other copyright works, e.g. musical and literary
- films – video footage, films, broadcasts, and cable programs.

Duration of copyright

The US copyright laws are promulgated in Title 17 of the US Code. In the United States, in general, for scholarship published after 1 January 1978 authors are given copyright protection of the work for their lifetime plus 70 years following their death.[12] If a work was published prior to 1 January 1978 then it may or may not be in the public domain, depending on whether proper mandatory filings were made with the US Copyright Office. One would have to consult with the US Copyright Office or a copyright attorney to determine if such filings were appropriately completed. Many variations and exceptions to the durations of copyright exist: to learn more about other possible durations consult 17 USC[13] or the US Copyright Office. Additionally, some exceptions apply to copyright rules when a work is to be used for purposes such as teaching, fair use, preservation, or replacement. Most of these exceptions are located in Title 17 of the US Code, sections 107, 108, 109(a) and (c), and 110(1) and (2). Librarians can also locate copyright exceptions in the Digital Millennium Copyright Act, section 112.

In the United Kingdom the duration of copyright is as follows.

- In general, copyright for literary, dramatic, musical, and artistic works lasts for 70 years from the end of the calendar year in which the last author of the work passes away.[14]
- For the duration of other specific works consult the UK Copyright Service webpage.[15]

Hypothetical scenario to understand copyright law

A hypothetical case is presented to understand what is and is not protected by copyright, and what exceptions may allow the use of a copyrighted material. Ms Simms is a teaching librarian who works at a government-funded university's general academic library (which may be in the United States or the United Kingdom). She has been asked to give several bibliographic instruction sessions for a history class. In planning this instruction Ms Simms decides to use websites, images located on the internet, links to other webpages, electronic articles discussing history, a video clip from YouTube, a clip from a historical movie, and a music clip. She would also like to place a book she owns personally on reserve for students to read, or perhaps place it on e-reserve. Does Ms Simms face any potential copyright problems?

In general a work is protected by US copyright law if it is original and fixed in tangible form.[16] Originality is usually defined as the creator being inspired to create the work, and the work having a modicum of creativity. Tangible format means print, digital, a sculpture... Thus the following materials are usually granted copyright protection:

- literary works
- musical works, including any accompanying works
- dramatic works, including any accompanying music
- pantomimes and choreographic works
- pictorial, graphic, and sculptural works
- motion pictures and other audio-visual works
- sound recordings
- architectural works.

Some items not granted copyright protection include:

- materials created by the US government (Government Printing Office), although some state and local government works are protected by copyright (e.g. in Oregon);[17] also, when determining if a work was published by the US government, one should take great care to decipher whether it was actually published by the Government Printing Office and not by a private publisher, which could catalyze some privately owned copyrights

- any idea, procedure, process, system, method of operation, concept, principle, or discovery[18]

- items in the public domain.[19]

The public domain is defined as works that are now out of copyright because their copyright term has expired, or copyright formalities (such as filings with the US Copyright Office) were not properly followed prior to 1978. For more information regarding terms of copyright consult the US Copyright Office website (*www.copyright.gov/*).

In our hypothetical case, are any of the materials Ms Simms wants to use in her class copyright protected? The information listed on a website, electronic articles, and the book will probably be considered literary works, depending on the type of content placed on the electronic venues. The YouTube video and the movie clip are sound recordings, and may be dramatic works. The images probably fall under the taxonomy of pictorial or graphic. The links lead to possible images or other literary works. Thus all the items Ms Simms desires to use, depending on whether they are older and in the public domain or more recent work, may be subject to some form of copyright protection. Before using these items in her pedagogy, Ms Simms should clarify what her jurisdiction's copyright laws mandate. If she determines any of the items are still under copyright protection, then is there a statutory exception that will allow her to utilize these in her pedagogy? Or should she seek permissions from the rightful copyright holder? If there are statutory exceptions available to permit use of these items, what are those acceptable exceptions?

Section 107 fair use in the United States

In the United States there are many statutory exceptions to a copyright holder's right to restrict the use of a creation. Section 107 of Title 17 is one of those exceptions, and provides for fair use. The fair-use exception allows the use of portions of copyrighted works when certain criteria are met. Whether these criteria are met is determined by the following weighted test.

- The purpose and character of the use, such as whether the primary reason for use is commercial or educational. The more the purpose is educational use, the greater chance it might be deemed fair use. Further, is the use transformative? Is it creating new expression or meaning? Is it establishing new information, design, use, or comprehension? Or is it simply just a duplicate copy utilized in your work? Is it being offered for criticism or critical analysis? The more transformative the use, the more likely it will be considered fair.

- The nature of the copyrighted work: was it created for scholarly educational purposes (e.g. a textbook), or was it created as a fictional work solely to generate money (e.g. a novel to be sold). If it is a scholarly work, this weighs in favor of fair use. Is the copyrighted work published or unpublished? If the work is published, your use of it is more likely to be deemed fair. The less use made of an unpublished work is often deemed better. The more factual (rather than creative) the work being copied, the more its use is weighted in favor of fair use.

- The amount of the work utilized in relation to the copyrighted work as a whole (e.g. was one chapter copied for use, two chapters, the entire work?). In general, the lesser amount of a work used, the more likely it is to be deemed fair use.

- The effect of the use upon the potential market for the copyrighted work. The less of a potential effect on the market, the more likely it is deemed fair use.[20]

Thus if Ms Simms wants to copy and make accessible a portion of an article during her teaching, in the United States she must ponder the following.

- What is the purpose of her use of this article? Is such use educational? If so, this weighs in her favor for a fair-use exception. Is her use transformational? Has her use created new information or insights so it is deemed transformational? Is her use serving a unique group of individuals who otherwise may not have access to these materials? If so, her right to use such material may be more likely to be deemed fair. Does the use involve criticism? If so, this weighs in favor of fair use as well.

- What is the nature of this article? Is it published and is it educational? If so, this may weigh in her favor. If the article was unpublished and created for commercial usage, this would probably weigh against her fair use. In general, the more one uses of an unpublished work, the more likely a court may hold such use is not fair. Is the work factual, or more of a fictional creative work? The more factual the information presented in the work, the heavier this weighs in favor of fair use.

- How much of an article or other item is Ms Simms utilizing? If she wants to use a small excerpt (a lot of US libraries adopt the policy of only allowing 10 percent usage or less of an article or book, although this percentage is not mandated by law), this may weigh in her favor when arguing fair use. If she wants to use all or half of the article, this may be eschewed under section 107; although, under fair use, if she is utilizing ten articles in total for her pedagogy, copying one full text of these ten total articles may be considered fair. There is not a general 10 percent rule listed in American statutory or judicial law. However, over the years many university libraries have adopted a policy that it is fair use when one copies one chapter out of a book with ten chapters, or one article placed on reserve when ten articles are used in an academic term (and there are no conflicting licensing agreements). Again, such a 10 percent standard is developed library policy, not black-letter law.

- What is the potential effect on the market? The lesser the effect on the potential market, the better.

Therefore, under section 107, Ms Simms may be able to copy or scan and provide access to one small excerpt of the article and book, and provide access to small excerpts of the video clips, as long as the clip is shown for educational purposes. Ms Simms could use a section 107 fair-use analysis for each of the items she wishes to use in her class.

Everyone must decide on their own whether their use is considered fair or not, based on evaluating all four factors. When in doubt, ask for permission from the copyright holder, or consult a copyright attorney licensed to practice in your jurisdiction.

What Ms Simms should take from this is that if she wants to copy some of the books, articles, or website then she should follow a few guidelines.

- She needs to ensure her use is transformational and educational; possibly critical of the work used.

- It would be wise to utilize published works. This weighs in the favor of fair use when using factual rather than creative and fictional works.

- She may want to check with her library to learn what its policy is on the normal percentage of items that may be used.

- It would also behoove Ms Simms to read the pertinent copyright statutes located in her jurisdiction and then put any questions she has to her academy legal counsel or scholarly communications officer.

To provide further clarification to the concept of fair use, the following gives a glimpse of how various civil courts in the United States have interpreted this doctrine. Some cases have used the fair-use test to weigh the utilization of copyrighted works.

Deemed fair use

In *Hustler Magazine, Inc. v. Moral Majority*,[21] Jerry Falwell made over 100,000 copies of one page that disparaged him in *Hustler* magazine. He then distributed these pages for a commercial purpose. Despite his monetary motives, the federal district court held such use to be fair because only one page was used, and such use did not weaken the potential market for this magazine issue. If anything, it probably raised the potential commercial value of the issue and increased the market. The court here focused on the third and fourth prongs of the fair-use test, the proportion used and the potential effect on the market, and deemed this usage fair.

Deemed not fair use

In *Love v. Kwitny*[22] an individual copied more than half of a work-in-progress manuscript and used it as potential evidence to suggest a person was attempting to overthrow the Iranian government. The court in this case focused on the third prong of fair use and reasoned that too substantial a portion of the manuscript had been copied and used (in this case much more than 10 percent of the document). Also, looking at the second prong of fair use, the court noted that the work was unpublished. It is always a good rule of thumb to use the least amount possible of an unpublished work.

In another case, *Nation* magazine printed many excerpts from President Ford's unpublished memoirs. *Nation* released these excerpts just before the Ford manuscript was published. The court in this case again focused on the second, third, and fourth prongs of fair use, and deemed that since the copyrighted work was unpublished, too much of the work was taken by the subsequent magazine issue. In other words, *Nation* stole the heart of President Ford's work. Further, the magazine greatly affected the potential market for his memoir, and it was therefore a violation of fair use.[23]

In *Basic Books, Inc. v. Kinko's Graphics Corp.* a US district court held that it was not fair use for a copy shop to photocopy book chapters or full-text articles and sell them to students. The court reasoned that performing such actions was greatly detrimental to the potential market of the publishers of these materials; in essence, too much information was copied (5–30 percent of each item was being copied – third prong), and the primary purpose for the copying was commercial, not educational (first prong). Further, such use was not transformational.[24]

UK fair-dealing exceptions

In the United Kingdom Ms Simms needs to be cognizant that her desired use of musical recordings, paintings, e-periodicals, and films is subject to copyright protections. May she still use these materials when teaching in the United Kingdom? To answer that question, let us determine if the United Kingdom offers any exceptions to these protections.

The United Kingdom does not recognize the American fair-use exception for copyrighted works. Instead, it implements a fair-dealing standard, which allows the use of copyrighted works under six circumstances.

- The work is utilized for research and private study for a non-commercial purpose, the original creator/creators must be given proper attribution, and the copies must not be made accessible to a great number of individuals.

- The copies are made for instruction or examination (literary, dramatic, musical, or artistic work or a sound recording, film, or broadcast). In granting such use the copying must be done by a student or an instructor, the copying may not be completed by a reprographic purpose, the original creator/creators must be given proper attribution, and the use must be for a non-commercial purpose.

- The copies are made for criticism or review. One may copy some portion of a work for criticism or review if the work is made available to the public, the original creator/creators are given proper attribution, and the material quoted is coupled with actual criticism or review. Additionally, the material quoted may not exceed an amount necessary for such criticism or review.

- The copies are made for news reporting, the work copied is not a photograph, the original creator/creators are acknowledged, and the amount copied is not more than is necessary for the news reporting.

- Copying occurs as an incidental inclusion where part of one work is unintentionally included in another. The incidental inclusion of a work in an artistic work, sound recording, film, or broadcast is not an infringement.

- Copying occurs in creating accessibility for someone with a visual impairment.

These fair-dealing exceptions are listed and described on the UK Copyright Service webpage.[25]

Fair dealing in the United Kingdom appears to be a bit more restrictive than is fair use in the United States. Further, the fair-dealing exceptions appear not to be a weighted test, as is the fair-use test in the United States. Thus, in the United Kingdom, Ms Simms's use of certain materials may be more restricted. For example, under the second prong of fair dealing she may be able to show a portion of a film, painting, or text by justifying this production under instruction to her students, or perhaps under the third prong for criticism and review in a classroom setting. However, Ms Simms, or anyone else wanting to use any item in the United Kingdom based on a theory of fair dealing, should seek guidance from individuals at the UK Parliament (*www.parliament.uk/*) or the UK Copyright Service (*www.copyrightservice.co.uk/copyright/*). Ms Simms should seek advice from legal counsel (a barrister or solicitor) or a scholarly communications officer located at her academy regarding what items are permissibly used in the United Kingdom and what items cannot be used for pedagogical purposes.

Digital excerpts on e-reserve and licensing agreements

Ms Simms also wants to place digital excerpts from electronic articles on e-reserve. Since this would be for an educational purpose, the articles have been published, and as long as the excerpts are small (again, consult with a librarian cognizant of the policy regarding how much of an item may be placed on an e-reserve system), then Ms Simms may have a good argument for such use of these items. However, a recent case held that even if digital excerpts of books placed on e-reserve are small, they may still violate licensing agreements if the librarians have contracted to pay for use of digital excerpts in such agreements.[26] Thus Ms Simms must be aware of what her university or library has contracted for in regard to the licensing agreement and what it mandates regarding use of digital excerpts placed on e-reserve. In other words, if an academy has a pre-existing licensing agreement specifying that members of the academy access journal articles only through an electronic database, then librarians should only access those articles via a database and not place excerpts of them on e-reserves. Further, if a university has contracted for a pre-existing license that mandates members of the academy may only post small excerpts (a certain percentage of an item) of articles found in those databases to e-reserves, then members should only place such excerpts in e-reserves (and the librarians should determine how the licensing agreement specifically defines 'small excerpts'). Thus, no matter in what jurisdiction Ms Simms lives, she should consult with her academy and learn what its licensing agreements mandate about the use of electronic articles prior to using these items in her pedagogy.

Other US exceptions to copyrights

Section 109(c) exception

In the United States, Ms Simms may also be able to locate an exception to copyright under section 109(c) of Title 17, which states that once a copyright holder authorizes the release of lawfully made copies of a work, the subsequent buyer may display this work in public or at a place of work as he or she pleases.[27] Thus Ms Simms may show the book she purchased to students in her class without committing copyright infringement. Further, the historical piece of art she wants to show the students may be displayed to them or to the entire university community under section 109(c), as long as she has legally obtained a lawfully made copy. Thus Ms Simms may display for her students both the lawfully obtained book and the artwork.

The case of *Wiley v. Kirtsaeng* to be decided by the US Supreme Court in 2013 may significantly alter this section 109(c) exception. In this case, a graduate student from Thailand attending school in the United States began to purchase textbooks from abroad and sell them for a more expensive price in the United States. Wiley filed a lawsuit against Kirtsaeng in a US district court alleging copyright infringement, claiming his purchase of these books did not equate to a 'lawfully obtained book'. A jury in this case agreed with Wiley's argument of copyright infringement and asked Kirtsaeng to pay Wiley damages in the amount of US$75,000 (£46,762.98) per infringed work. Kirtsaeng appealed this decision to the US Second Circuit Court of Appeals, and this appellate court upheld the district court's decision. Kirtsaeng then appealed to the US Supreme Court.[28] A decision on this case should be given by the Supreme Court in or about June 2013. If the Supreme Court upholds the Second Circuit's decision, this could impact how American libraries may lend, display, transfer, and gift books and other tangible items. Further at issue in this case is how section 602(a)(1) of the Copyright Act meshes with section 109(c), which prohibits the importation of a copyrighted work without the authority of the copyright's owner.[29] Of course, the Supreme Court could deliver a narrow holding and attempt to exclude possible negative effects on libraries and museums located in the United States. One will have to wait until the court rules for further guidance on this issue.

Section 110(1): face-to-face instruction in the United States

In the United States, section 110(1) of Title 17 in the US Code may give Ms Simms the best argument to use some of the works she wants to share with her class. Section 110(1) conveys that instructors of non-profit educational institutions may show performances and displays of various types of works in a classroom.[30] These types of works may consist of portions of video clips for educational purposes, music, recitation or poetry, or plays... The caveat to this exception is that the performance or display of such works must be part of the instructional activities, they may not be for entertainment, and the work performed or displayed must be lawfully obtained.

Due to this exception, if Ms Simms's video and music clips, websites, and images were lawfully obtained and are shown within a related instructional activity, then she may be able to display them to her students. Yet this section does not give her permission to copy items in any amount for her class. To make additional copies, Ms Simms could rely on and evaluate the section 107 four-factor analysis of fair use.

Section 110(2) TEACH Act

If Ms Simms is offering instruction via an online course management system such as Blackboard in the United States, then section 110(2) also offers some exceptions that may allow her to display and utilize copyrighted materials. This section is often referred to by its acronym, TEACH (Technology, Education, and Copyright Harmonization). It does not offer as broad exceptions as does section 110(1), which governs face-to-face instruction. However, section 110(2) allows instructors to utilize:

- performances of non-dramatic literary works
- performances of non-dramatic musical works
- performances of any other works, including dramatic works and audio-visual works, but only in 'reasonable and limited portions'
- display of any work in an amount comparable to that which is typically displayed in the course of a live classroom.[31]

Note that under the TEACH Act only reasonable and limited portions of audio-visual works may be displayed, and such a performance or display must occur at the direction of, or under the actual supervision of, an instructor as an integral part of a class session offered as a regular part of the systematic mediated instructional activities. So can Ms Simms get her pedagogical point across to her students when only being allowed to display a limited portion of her historical film (possibly only a certain number of minutes of film)? What does 'reasonable and limited portions' mean? The TEACH Act does not clearly define the meaning of this phrase. Although we do not yet have clear guidance from the courts regarding how much of 'performances of other works' is considered 'reasonable and limited', perhaps the future will offer a clearer picture of what this phrase means.

In order to use the TEACH Act and grant their faculty, students, and staff specific copyright exceptions, universities must comply with certain statutory mandates. These include institutional requirements such as:

- the university must be an accredited non-profit educational institution
- the university must create and 'institute policies regarding copyright'
- the university must create and 'provide informational materials regarding copyright'
- such informational materials must convey how to comply with copyright, and be disseminated to students, faculty, and staff
- the university must convey to students that materials used in connection with the course may be subject to copyright protection.[32]

The TEACH Act also requires universities to limit access to course materials to only those students enrolled, and it must ensure students know not to disseminate the materials to other individuals not enrolled in the course. It must prevent retention of the work in accessible form by recipients of the transmission from the transmitting body or institution for longer than the class session, and prevent conduct that could reasonably be expected to interfere with technological measures used by copyright owners to prevent such retention or unauthorized further dissemination.[33] Thus it would behoove Ms Simms to stay abreast of current copyright law and policy, ensure her students are cognizant of such policies and laws, and make certain the university for which she works has met all necessary criteria to obtain the luxuries under the TEACH Act.

Cornell University Law School has a helpful website giving further requirements of the TEACH Act and a more detailed description of the Act.[34]

Thus section 110(2) gives Ms Simms some flexibility if she is providing instruction via an online venue such as Blackboard and her university is meeting all the necessary requirements mandated by the TEACH Act. If her instruction falls within this exception, she may be able to show a portion of her film, she should probably complete a fair-use analysis to determine whether she may utilize any digital images, and she may be free to link to websites or articles stored in electronic databases to which her institution subscribes via a licensing agreement. When linking to websites, she should probably link to the homepage of the site and instruct her students to investigate the deeper links on each webpage. Linking to the homepage of trusted websites will prevent possible unintended infringement.

UK exceptions to copyright for educational purposes

Classroom use in the United Kingdom

The United Kingdom defines educational establishments as any school, college, or university offering further or higher education. Under UK law, such educational establishments may be able to show a video or DVD to students, and may not need a license from owners of the copyrights if certain requirements are met.

- The video/DVD must be shown in an educational establishment.

- An 'educational establishment' is defined in copyright law as including any school (colleges offering further or higher education and universities are also 'educational establishments'). 'School' has the meaning given by education legislation:
  - in England and Wales, the Education Act 1996
  - in Scotland, the Education (Scotland) Act 1962 (including approved schools under the Social Work (Scotland) Act 1968)
  - in Northern Ireland, the Education and Libraries (Northern Ireland) Order 1986.

- The audience must only consist of students, teachers, and others connected with the activities of the school

- The displaying of the DVD or film must be for an instructional purpose.[35]

Anyone seeking to use these types of materials in the United Kingdom should consult the UK Intellectual Property Office (*www.ipo.gov.uk/*), the UK Parliament (*www.parliament.uk/*), or the UK Copyright Service (*www.copyrightservice.co.uk/*). Additionally, anyone wanting to show a DVD or video to students in the United Kingdom should consult their academy's legal counsel (such as a barrister or solicitor) or scholarly communications officer.

The United Kingdom and the TEACH Act

The United Kingdom does not offer copyright exceptions under any statute similar to the US TEACH Act. To be able to show videos to college or secondary students in the

United Kingdom, one would have to use the copyright exceptions regarding UK educational establishments listed above.[36]

The United Kingdom and circumvention of CSS

In the United Kingdom a CSS (content scrambling system) is referred to as digital rights management protections, and they are legal. However, a person believing he or she has the right to make lawful use of copyrighted materials via a copyrighted exception may request a workaround. If the copyright owner does not issue a workaround one may make a complaint to the secretary of state, who will then consider this complaint.[37] Thus in the United States and the United Kingdom lawful measures may be available to show a video or film in an educational setting that has been restricted by a content scrambling system. However, before attempting to show an educational video or film that has been restricted in this way, you should first consult with legal counsel at your academy, or with a private attorney, barrister, or solicitor.

Creative Commons

In many ways copyright law does not address every fathomable situation in the digital world. As a result, some non-profit groups have proffered licenses on their own on top of copyright protection. For example, Creative Commons (CC) licenses have been developed to address the needs of creators in digital venues.[38] CC licenses allow authors and creators residing all around the world to retain copyright of their works, while affording the public an opportunity to distribute, copy, and otherwise utilize these works. The licenses are built upon general copyright law, and are recognized internationally. They offer the public more liberal uses of works by granting them non-exclusive licenses. The first few versions of the CC licenses (1.0, 2.0, 2.5) were drafted to comply with US copyright law. The 3.0 version licenses were created to comply with relevant international treaties, thus they are more portable across various countries. The Creative Commons website states that the 4.0 set of licenses was due to be released in or about December 2012, although this has not yet happened.[39]

There are six general types of 3.0 licenses from which a creator may choose.

- *Attribution – CC BY.* The attribution CC BY license affords a subsequent user the opportunity to distribute, remix, amend, and add to or delete portions of the original work. The revised work may be used for commercial or non-profit purposes. However, the new user must credit the original creator for the original work. This is the most liberal of the six CC licenses.[40]

- *Attribution NoDerivs – CC BY-ND.* This type of license allows a subsequent user to redistribute for commercial and non-commercial motives, but the original work may not be amended or revised in any guise. Further, each subsequent user of the work must give credit to the original owner.[41]

- *Attribution Non-Commercial ShareAlike – CC BY-NC-SA.* This type of license permits subsequent users to amend, revise, and build upon the original work. Each revision, however, must be used for a non-commercial purpose. Each subsequent user must also give credit to the original creator, and must license his or her new creation in the same manner as the original creator. Therefore, each subsequent creator shall license his or her rendition with a CC BY-NC-SA license, allow other subsequent users to tweak, amend, and build upon the new creation for non-commercial purposes, and license their new creations under identical terms.[42]

- *Attribution ShareAlike – CC BY-SA.* The CC BY-SA license allows successive users to amend, revise, and build upon the original work for non-commercial or commercial purposes, as long as they give credit to the original inventor and license their new creation with a CC BY-SA license. It is often referred to as a 'Copyleft' free and open source software license. Wikipedia was licensed with this type of CC license.[43]

- *Attribution Non-Commercial – CC BY-NC.* This type of license allows users to amend, revise, and build upon the original work for non-commercial purposes. Each ensuing user must not use his or her rendition for commercial purposes, must give the original creator credit, and does not have to license his or her new version in the same manner as the original creator.[44]

- *Attribution Non-Commercial NoDerivs – CC BY-NC-ND.* This is the strictest license offered by CC. It only allows others to download your work and share it. While downloading and sharing a work users must credit the original owner, and are restricted from using this original work for commercial purposes or amending or building upon it in any manner.

How do CC licenses affect librarians?

CC licenses[45] potentially give teaching librarians more autonomy to make liberal use of original works licensed with a CC license. For example, a librarian giving bibliographic instruction to college freshmen may locate a digital annotated bibliographic guide regarding Russian literature. Under fair use, the librarian may only be able to use and distribute a small portion of this guide to students to augment his or her instruction. However, if the creator of this guide licensed it with a CC BY-NC or CC BY-NC-SA license, then the subsequent user, the librarian, may revise, amend, and build upon the Russian literature bibliography, and use it for pedagogical purposes without fear of copyright infringement.

Additionally, if the original creator of the Russian annotated bibliography licensed the work with a CC BY-SA, the librarian may revise, amend, and build upon the work; distribute it to students and use it for pedagogical purposes; and even use his or her new rendition of the annotated bibliography for commercial purposes. Thus CC licenses afford librarians more liberal uses of works, more autonomy in the manner in which they choose to utilize them, and freedom to implement them in pedagogical or commercial endeavors absent of the fear of infringing upon original creators' copyright protection. Such liberal usage of works promotes higher levels of thought in students and thus the freedom to synthesize new information, and is more in line with the purpose of promoting scientific and creative discoveries and creations.[46]

Other information about Creative Commons

Currently the most common element used by CC licensors is the non-commercial aspect. If works are amended by subsequent users, most CC licensors prefer this modification is not for commercial purposes. The most prolific users of

CC licenses are hobbyists. However, many universities are now experimenting with the benefits of Creative Commons by encouraging their faculty to create works or create and utilize courseware and license them with CC licenses. Coates[47] illustrates how Massachusetts Institute of Technology's Open Course Ware (OCW) program has benefited many faculty, students, and individuals affiliated with MIT by utilizing the CC Attribution Non-Commercial ShareAlike license.

- Seventy-five percent of MIT's faculty had published courses on OCW.
- Educators at MIT and other universities recycle and reuse the course content.
- Sixty-two percent combined OCW materials with other content.
- A large percentage of students feel this open courseware benefits them.

Can Creative Commons benefit Ms Simms?

Creative Commons can benefit Ms Simms in that along with her fair-use options, section 110(1), and her other possible copyright exceptions, she now may seek out historical films, images, websites, and other information licensed under a CC license. In locating any of these materials she may now share them with her class, and possibly even tweak or modify them and have her class license them if the CC license allows for such use.

A number of academies now use CC licenses for open courseware, and it may be possible to learn from their experiences.

- MIT – *http://ocw.mit.edu/help/*.
- Stanford – *http://creativecommons.org/weblog/entry/10767*.
- Berklee College of Music, Boston – *http://creativecommons.org/press-releases/entry/3900*.
- Open Course Library created by Washington State Board for Community and Technical Colleges – *http://sbctc.edu/college/_e-elearningprojects.aspx*.
- University of Michigan – *www.lib.umich.edu/news/mlibrary-adopts-new-creative-commons-license*. Michigan is utilizing a CC BY license for content: it first adopted a CC BY-NC license in 2008, but decided in 2010 to implement a CC BY license.
- University of Cambridge Language Centre – *www.langcen.cam.ac.uk/opencourseware/index.html*. The open courseware uses a CC BY-NC-ND license.
- University of Massachusetts, Boston – *http://ocw.umb.edu/*. The open courseware uses a CC BY-NC-SA license,
- University of Notre Dame – *http://ocw.nd.edu/*. The open courseware uses a CC BY-NC-SA, but allows use of other licenses. Other faculty are encouraged to use and distribute material.

Teaching librarians may also wish to access images licensed with CC licenses.[48]

SPARC Addendum

Another tool that can help authors of articles retain their copyrights is the SPARC Addendum, created by the Scholarly Publishing and Academic Resources Coalition

(SPARC – *www.arl.org/sparc/*). This addendum is a legal tool one may submit to a publisher in concert with a publishing agreement. It acts as a pre-existing license that allows an author of an article to retain his or her copyrights, such as the right to reproduce, distribute, create derivatives, display, and perform his or her tangible article. The addendum grants the publisher a non-exclusive right simultaneously to publish the article, disseminate it in print or electronic format, and receive proper attribution from anyone who uses it. The SPARC Addendum is based on a CC BY license.

The SPARC Addendum benefits authors in this regard:

- it allows them to retain the rights they want to keep
- it permits them to use and modify their work without restriction
- it increases access for education and research
- it allows them to receive proper attribution when their work is used
- it allows them to deposit into an electric repository.

The SPARC Addendum benefits publishers by:

- granting them a non-exclusive right to publish and distribute the work
- allowing them still to receive ample monetary benefits
- allowing them to mandate proper attribution and citation
- granting them the right to use the work in alternative formats and future collections.

Thus a teaching librarian could utilize this tool in a class project that instructs students to draft an article on a specific topic. At the end of the term, students could submit the article to a publisher in concert with the SPARC Addendum. If the article is accepted for publication, then each student, the instructor, and any other co-authors retain their copyrights and may use this article in the future without restriction.[49]

Images and US copyright

Many dangers exist in cyberspace regarding utilizing images and linking to content. As more librarians implement links and images in their pedagogy, this exposes them and the institutions for which they work to copyright infringement. For example, Ms Simms wants to use images and links to websites pertaining to history in her current pedagogical assignment. However, what if the pages to which she links contain infringing materials? Or the creator of the images to which she links has not approved classroom use? If such a scenario unfolds, is Ms Simms liable for direct or indirect copyright infringement? Direct copyright infringement is defined as when a user places copyrighted information, images, or other materials directly on his or her own webpage without gaining permission. Indirect infringement in this scenario consists of a user linking to another webpage that displays infringing material.[50] Thus if Ms Simms wants to use an image to serve as a link, she should consider the following as viable options.

- Link to the homepages of websites, not the deeper-level pages.
- If a librarian wants students to access information on deeper-level pages, orally convey to them that they need to click deeper into the website.

- Only link to sites that are not likely to contain infringing material. Link to the British Museum's site, not Jimmy's favorite art.

- Before linking to a site, investigate it: look to see if the site states it has received permissions from authors, creators... to post information

- Do not use images as links; use text for links instead.

- If you are going to use images for links, ensure they are licensed with a CC license that allows you to use them in this way, such as a CC BY, CC BY-ND, CC BY-NC SA, CC BY-SA, or CC BY-NC.

- Look for images licensed with CC licenses (*http:// creativecommons.org/image/*).

- If an image allows you to use it as a link (e.g. CC license), ensure you give the original creator proper credit if the license requires this.

- If the original creator did not license the image with a CC license, then obtain permission from this original creator to use the image as a link.

- Post a notice by the link or at the bottom of your guide stating that you have permission to use the image as a link.

Copyright tips

If you have a copyrighted work or an excerpt of a work you want to use, remember that you have an arsenal of tools within the scope of the law, no matter in what jurisdiction you reside.

- First, determine whether it is copyrighted. It may be in the public domain due to its age, or a lack of the creator properly renewing copyright. In the United States, take a look at the US Copyright Registry (*www.copyright.gov/ records/*). However, remember that just because a work is not registered, it does not mean that it is not still under copyright protection. Also consider contacting a US copyright attorney for advice. In the United Kingdom, determine whether the item is under copyright, refer to the UK Copyright Service, and consult a barrister or solicitor.

- Remember that in limited circumstances one may utilize copyrighted works for educational purposes. In the United Kingdom, consult the Intellectual Property Office (*www.ipo.gov.uk/types/copy/c-other/c-other-faq/c-other-faq-excep/c-other-faq-excep-vid.htm*) and the Copyright Service (*www.copyrightservice.co.uk/copyright/p27_work_of_others*) for proper use of a copyrighted material in an educational setting. In the United States, consider the fair-use exception, section 109, the TEACH Act, or section 110(1) for possible limited usage of copyrighted materials.

- If no exception seems to fit, consult the owner of the copyrighted material and ask for permission or to pay a licensing fee to use the work.

- Consult Creative Commons to locate items that are licensed for further use in an educational arena.

Conclusion

In conclusion, teaching librarians such as Ms Simms should keep abreast of what actions constitute defamatory conduct, copyright infringement, plagiarism, and other possible legal pitfalls. These librarians should offer brief instruction to their students at the commencement of an academic term to inculcate students with what constitutes legal conduct and what conduct could get them into legal hot water. For example, a librarian could use the first class session to demonstrate what is appropriate information to post on Facebook, Google+, Mindomo, a website, Second Life… and what content would be considered plagiarism, a violation of another's copyright, or defamation. The librarian could further demonstrate how to link properly to YouTube or Vimeo to avoid indirect copyright infringement. Then occasionally throughout the semester the librarian could give supplemental instruction when he or she believes a student may have posted improper content to a Web 2.0 or 3.0 tool.

Notes

1. Restatement (Second) of Torts, §§ 559 et seq. (2010).
2. *Pitale v. Holstine*, No. 11 C 00921, 2012 WL 638755 (N.D. Ill., 27 February 2012).
3. *Bell Atl. v. Twombly*, 550 US 544, 555 (2007).
4. *Madison v. Frazier*, 539 F.3d 646, 653 (7th Cir., 2008).
5. See *Pope v. Chronicle Pub. Co.*, 95 F.3d 607, 616 (7th Cir., 1996); *Kolegas v. Heftel Broad. Corp.*, 607 N.E.2d 201, 209 (Ill., 1992); *Moriarty v. Greene*, 732 N.E.2d, 225, 241 (Ill. App.Ct, 2000).
6. *Sweezy v. New Hampshire*, 354 US 234 (1957). See also Watts, W. (2011) '*Butler University v. John Doe*: a new challenge to academic freedom and shared governance', *AAUP Journal of Academic Freedom*, 2: 1–26.
7. Infodocket (2013) 'Press roundup: Mellen Press libel lawsuits vs. librarian and McMaster University'; available at: *www.infodocket.com/2013/02/11/press-and-document-roundup-mellen-press-libel-lawsuit-vs-dale-askey-and-mcmaster-university-librarian/* (accessed: 20 February 2013).

8. UK Parliament (2013) 'Defamation Act 2013'; available at: *http://services.parliament.uk/bills/2012-13/defamation.html* (accessed: 30 January 2013).

9. Barbee, D. (2012) 'Judge throws out $14 million jury award in online libel case', *Star Telegram*, 13 June; available at: *www.star-telegram.com/2012/06/13/4027734/judge-throws-out-14-million-jury.html* (accessed: 15 February 2013).

10. US Copyright Act, 17 USC, § 106.

11. UK Copyright Service; available at: *www.copyrightservice.co.uk/copyright/p01_uk_copyright_law* (accessed: 25 February 2013).

12. US Copyright Act, 17 USC, § 302.

13. Ibid., § 302 et seq.

14. UK Copyright Service, note 11 above.

15. Ibid.

16. US Copyright Act, 17 USC, § 102(a).

17. Ibid., § 105.

18. Ibid., § 102(a).

19. Ibid.

20. Ibid., § 107.

21. *Hustler Magazine, Inc. v. Moral Majority, Inc.*, 606 F. Supp. 1526 (C.D. Cal., 1985).

22. *Love v. Kwitny*, 772 F. Supp. 1367 (S.D. N.Y., 1989).

23. *Harper & Row Publishers, Inc. v. Nation Magazine*, 471 U.S. 539 (1985).

24. *Basic Books, Inc. v. Kinko's Graphics Corp.*, 758 F. Supp. 1522 (S.D. N.Y., 1991).

25. UK Copyright Service; available at: *www.copyrightservice.co.uk/copyright/p27_work_of_others* (accessed: 25 February 2013).

26. *Cambridge Univ. Press v. Becker*, 863 F. Supp.2d 1190 (N.D. Ga., 2012).

27. US Copyright Act, 17 USC, § 109(c).

28. *Kirtsaeng v. John Wiley & Sons, Inc.*, 132 S.Ct 1905 (2012).

29. US Copyright Act, 17 USC, § 602(a)(1).

30. Ibid., § 110(1).

31. Ibid., § 110(2).

32. Ibid., § 110(2)(d).

33. Ibid., § 110(2).

34. Cornell University Law School, Legal Information Institute; available at: *www.law.cornell.edu/uscode/text/17/110* (accessed: 26 February 2013).

35. UK Intellectual Property Office; available at: *www.ipo.gov. uk/types/copy/c-other/c-other-faq/c-other-faq-excep/c-other-faq-excep-vid.htm* (accessed: 12 February 2013).

36. Ibid.

37. UK Intellectual Property Office; available at: *www.ipo.gov. uk/types/copy/c-other/c-other-faq/c-other-faq-excep/c-other-faq-excep-drm.htm* (accessed: 12 February 2013).

38. Coates, J. (2007) 'Creative Commons – the next generation: Creative Commons license use five years on', *SCRIPTed*, 4(1): 72.

39. Creative Commons; available at: *http://creativecommons.org/* (accessed: 23 February 2013).

40. Ibid.

41. Ibid.

42. Ibid.

43. Ibid.

44. Ibid.

45. Creative Commons, 'About the licenses'; available at: *http:// creativecommons.org/licenses/* (accessed: 23 February 2013).

46. US Constitution, Art. 1, § 8, cl. 8.

47. Coates, note 38 above.

48. Creative Commons, 'Images'; available at: *http:// creativecommons.org/image/* (accessed: 23 February 2013).

49. ARL, 'Addendum to publication agreement'; available at: *www.arl.org/sparc/bm~doc/Access-Reuse_Addendum.pdf* (accessed: 23 February 2013).

50. Hoffmann, G.M. (2005) *Copyright in Cyberspace 2*. London: Neal-Schuman Publishers.

Appendix: useful websites and other links

General

AccessMyLibrary *www.gale.cengage.com/apps/aml/CollegeLibrary/*

Adobe Connect *www.adobe.com/products/adobeconnect.html*

Air Video *www.inmethod.com/air-video/index.html;jsessionid=4B1A5F4BA6F0650C7EFEC8E4F9DE84BE*

ArticleSearch *https://itunes.apple.com/us/app/articlesearch/id401914624?mt=8*

Attendance2 *www.dave256apps.com/attendance/*

Boopsie *www.boopsie.com*

BuildAnApp *www.buildanapp.com/home*

Camtasia *www.techsmith.com/camtasia.html*

Catch *https://catch.com*

Dropbox *https://www.dropbox.com/*

EasyBib *www.easybib.com*

EverNote *http://evernote.com*

Google Calendar *https://www.google.com/calendar/*

Google Drive *https://drive.google.com/*

Google Sites *https://sites.google.com/*

Inspiration Maps *https://itunes.apple.com/us/app/inspiration-maps/id510173686?mt=8*

Instapaper *www.instapaper.com*

Kindle *www.amazon.com/gp/feature.html?ie=UTF8&docId=1000493771*

LibAnywhere *www.libanywhere.com*

LibGuides *http://springshare.com/libguides/ http://libguides.com/community.php?m=i&ref=www.libguides.com*

Mindomo *www.mindomo.com/*

Moodle *https://moodle.org/*

MyAppBuilder *http://myappbuilder.com*

Padlet *http://padlet.com*

PB Works *http://pbworks.com/*

Pocket *http://getpocket.com*

Qik *http://qik.com*

Second Life *http://secondlife.com/*

Skype *www.skype.com/en/*

SlideShare *www.slideshare.net/*

Trello *https://trello.com*

Wetpaint Wikis in Education *http://wikisineducation.wetpaint.com/*

Wikispaces *www.wikispaces.com/*

YouTube *www.youtube.com/*

Websites related to legal issues

The following links are helpful in locating and accessing current copyright laws.

United States

US Copyright Office   *www.copyright.gov/*
This site offers information about general copyright questions, scenarios, publications, fees, licenses, recording, searching tips, domestic regulations, and international law.

US Copyright Office description of fair use   *www.copyright. gov/fls/fl102.html*

US legislative developments regarding copyright   *www. copyright.gov/legislation/*
This site describes the basics of fair use, and how to obtain general permissions from copyright holders.

US Copyright Clearance Center   *www.copyright.com/*

Stanford University   *http://fairuse.stanford.edu/primary_ materials/cases/index.html*
This site offers general guidance on basic copyrights, statutory copyright exceptions, and case law that has interpreted copyright statutes. The University of Stanford houses material about copyright and fair use, including US case law interpreting fair use.

FindLaw   *http://codes.lp.findlaw.com/uscode/17/1/107*
Details of 17 USC §107 (2010), the section delineating fair use in the United States.

United Kingdom

Intellectual Property Office *www.ipo.gov.uk/home.htm*
This site contains general information regarding patents, trademarks, designs, and copyright.

UK Copyright Service *www.copyrightservice.co.uk/*
This site provides information about copyright registration; solicitors, agents, and publishers; free educational fact sheets; and how to protect one's works.

Databases from which to access US copyright laws

Westlaw: Database name: US Copyrights; Database identifier: COPYRIGHTS
This database offers forms, case law, proposed legislation, session laws, and other materials related to intellectual property.

Westlaw: Database name: US Copyright Office Forms; Database identifier: COPYRIGHT-FRMS
US copyright forms.

Hein Online: Intellectual Property Law Collection library
This database contains current statutes, case law, and judicial interpretation regarding copyright.

Other sites

Creative Commons *http://creativecommons.org/*

Creative Commons images *http://creativecommons.org/image/*

Material licensed with Creative Commons licenses
http://search.creativecommons.org/
This website allows you to search for images, videos, text...
with CC licenses.

Flickr Creative Commons *www.flickr.com/creativecommons/*

SPARC *www.arl.org/sparc/*

Coalition of Open Access Policy Institutions *www.sparc.arl.org/about/COAPI/*
More information about the SPARC Addendum.

US Copyright Registry *www.copyright.gov/records/*

UK Parliament *www.parliament.uk/*

Index

CPSIA information can be obtained at www.ICGtesting.com
Printed in the USA
BVOW06s2122131215

430161BV00003B/37/P

9 781843 347330